THE WAY OF REAL WEALTH

Creating a Future
That Is Emotionally Satisfying,
Spiritually Fulfilling,
Financially Secure

Mark S. Waldman, Ph.D., CFP

ELEMENT
Shaftesbury, Dorset ● Rockport, Massachusetts
Brisbane, Queensland

© Mark Waldman 1993, published by arrangement
with the Hazelden Foundation

First published in 1993 by Hazelden Educational Materials

This edition published in Great Britain in 1995 by
Element Books Limited
Shaftesbury, Dorset SP7 8BP

Published in Australia in 1995 by
Element Books Limited
for Jacaranda Wiley Limited
33 Park Road, Milton, Brisbane 4064

Cover Design by Max Fairbrother
Design by Hazelden Educational Materials
Typeset by ABM Typographics Ltd., Hull
Printed and bound in Great Britain by BPC Paperbacks Ltd, Aylesbury, Bucks

British Library Cataloguing in Publication
data available

Library of Congress Cataloging in Publication
data available

ISBN 1-85230-641-6

THE WAY OF REAL WEALTH

About the author:

A financial planner since 1983, Mark Waldman hosts a weekly personal finance call-in show on WWRC radio in Washington, D.C. His listeners know him as "The Money Doctor." Waldman has conducted seminars entitled "Creating the Financial Future You Want" at the Omega Institute for Holistic Studies and is an adjunct professor at The American University in Washington, D.C. He received a Ph.D. in economics from the University of Florida in 1974.

This book is dedicated to the memory of my father,
Seymour B. Waldman,
and to my mother and my sister,
Marcella Waldman
and
Jane Sara Waldman.

Editor's note

The names of the people in this book who have shared their experiences have been changed. This book also includes some experiences that are composites taken from a group of people who have had similar experiences. In the last case, any resemblance to specific people or specific situations is accidental.

The following publishers and authors have granted us their
permission to use extracted quotations from copyrighted works:

From *Wiseguy* by Nicholas Pileggi. Copyright © 1985 by Pileggi Literary Properties, Inc. Reprinted by permission of Simon & Schuster, Inc.

CONTENTS

Contents

FOREWORD

No facet of contemporary life is more complicated than our relationship with money. Money affects every part of our lives, yet we are often unaware of how we're affected by this powerful network of beliefs, attitudes, and behavior.

Dr. Waldman shows how we have given money power over us and how this reinforces our lack of consciousness of how deeply money affects us. We may judge some effects to be positive and others negative, but his book explains that regardless of whether we like the results, patterned and habitual responses to life's challenges are a form of unconsciousness. They limit our freedom and restrict our spiritual growth.

The Way of Real Wealth gently guides us in examining how we think about and behave with money and how it can be used for a higher purpose: gaining inner freedom and direct contact with the Divine. At the same time, this book shows us how to achieve this while participating fully in daily life. This book illustrates that it is possible to fully engage all our talents and abilities while developing a deeper awareness of our thoughts, feelings, and behavior. Our daily life, then, can be a laboratory for personal and spiritual growth.

Through anecdotes from the author's experience as an economist and investment adviser and the use of teaching stories from a variety of religious traditions, *The Way of Real Wealth* illustrates the consequences of giving money control of our lives. When we think that something "out there" is making us feel the way we do—particularly when we depend on money for our security, self-image, and social persona—we give up responsibility for our growth and our lives. We minimize the possibility of meaningful change.

To reclaim ourselves, we must break through the network of attitudes, beliefs, and behavior that binds us to the past. We must understand our unique selves and lives, and we must follow that understanding to its roots to remove the hidden chains with which we have bound ourselves.

The Way of Real Wealth is a practical book. It includes detailed exercises designed to increase our awareness of our relationship with money. Other exercises help us discover what our true values are and what work would be most satisfying. Several chapters focus on discovering and using values that work in both the spiritual and financial realms.

The exercises give the reader a great deal of latitude. They help us discover our own path, rather than try to force a particular path on us. Doing these exercises can initiate a growth process that becomes self-sustaining, leading to a deeply personal experience of the essence of life. This is genuine spirituality that can flow from inside each of us.

Spirituality is the separation of the superficial from the essential. Spiritual work leads us to the essential within each of us, which in turn enables us to recognize the essential in others. Like calls out to like. Love calls out to love.

Nothing in our culture distracts us from the essential like money does. It is a powerful symbol for all the attachments that cloud our awareness, cover our hearts, and veil our eyes. *The Way of Real Wealth* shows us how to use money as a mirror, to see more clearly and to focus the light of self-awareness. As we do this, we gain a potent tool for learning to be *in* the material world, but not *of* it.

This book helps us experience life as a whole and to use that experience as a tool for self-transformation. Life has both horizontal and vertical dimensions: the former is our connection with each other and with things, and the latter is our connection with higher forms of awareness. The ideas in this book can lead readers to integrate these dimensions in whatever ways will be most useful to them.

In *The Way of Real Wealth,* Dr. Waldman guides rather than lectures. Real growth comes from within, and because each of us is different, our paths must also differ. He does not ask us to fit ourselves into boxes or types, nor does he give us prepackaged solutions to predigested problems. Dr. Waldman encourages us not to see ourselves as passive victims of our pasts and circumstances. This book offers us the tools to help us become more aware of our blocks and limitations, and then it helps us find the unique path that each of us must discover if we are to grow.

Many of us are working to improve our world. We want to build a world of peace, community, and fairness. But the problems we want to solve exist within us as well as in the world. If we want to find real and lasting solutions, we must first identify those problems and make those changes within ourselves. If we are filled with fear and anxiety, we worsen the worldly imbalances we want to redress. Only when we begin to become internally free do our actions start to generate the lasting external change that our hearts desire.

It is in acting on these internal changes that the spiritual and material overlap. Dr. Waldman shows us how to bring a new awareness to the personal and professional choices we make. By making these choices from the deepest part of ourselves rather than allowing society to dictate to us, each of us can become a powerful force for change.

No area of contemporary life cries out for as much attention yet goes as unaddressed as does our relationship with money. *The Way of Real Wealth* can help correct this massive lack of social attention. It offers us a valid tool for gaining inner freedom and spiritual growth.

The American University
Washington, D.C.

ABDUL AZIZ SAID
Professor of International Relations

ACKNOWLEDGMENTS

Writing this book has been a humbling as well as an exhilarating experience. I've become much more aware of the spiritual and intellectual debts I owe to many people. Some of them know me, some don't. Some helped me, others obstructed. I learned from them all.

Friends who have helped greatly over the years include Walter Drimer, Jane and Bataan Faigao, Tam Gibbs, Dr. Irving Goffman, Dr. Samuel Goldberger, Henry Gooch, Alan Levy, Tom Martin, Bill and Susan Ryder, Mickey Singer, Robert Smith, and Phil Tepperberg. There are others too numerous to mention. I honor all of them.

I'm particularly grateful to Reshad Feild for his instruction and guidance in many aspects of my life. During our time together, I learned a great deal about discerning the real from the imaginary. The seeds that time planted in me have continued to sprout and grow.

Dr. Abdul Aziz Said, professor of international relations, peace studies, and conflict resolution at the School of International Service of The American University in Washington, D.C., has been a special friend and loving guide for the last thirteen years. He's had the patience and integrity to avoid answering my questions, which has forced me to learn for myself. Through his heart, I can perceive faint images of how it's possible to be.

My agents Ling Lucas and Ed Vesneske Jr. played a special role in making this book a reality. Their support and suggestions made the project possible, the writing easier, and the end result better. Susan Meltsner helped with the book proposal.

Rebecca Post at Hazelden Educational Materials also helped in the development of this book. Her enthusiastic response to the manuscript helped enormously. Her caring editing made the work of rewriting easier. And her open, cooperative style made the book's production and marketing enjoyable.

Those who've helped have only added to the quality of the work. Any error or lack of clarity is mine.

INTRODUCTION

Money is so important to us! We live in a society where the amount of money we have affects almost every part of our lives. But perhaps the most surprising thing is that we don't take money more seriously than we do. After all, our hopes for the future, our fears, our anxieties, our dreams, the way we give and receive love, our relationship with power, our self-image, and our social persona are all powerfully related to what money means to us.

The ways we think about, feel about, and behave with money, whether it's ours or someone else's, reveal a great deal about us. If we could just see ourselves more clearly, we could start freeing ourselves of the limiting and self-defeating patterns of thought and behavior that we've carried with us all our lives.

Is This All There Is?

More! More! is the cry of a mistaken soul.
—William Blake

This book isn't about having it all. It's about spiritual growth, which has nothing to do with whether or not we get what we want in life. Spirituality doesn't mean adopting beliefs that make us feel better when we don't get what we want. It doesn't mean acting certain ways so others think we're spiritual. Spirituality means freeing ourselves from an ego-based view of ourselves and the world. It means allowing a different experience to enter our awareness.

That spiritual experience has been called God, Allah, Yahweh, Christ, Satchitananda, Buddha, Nature, Tao, Higher Power, The Great Spirit, and thousands of other names. The particular name isn't important. What is important is that we recognize the differences a spiritual understanding of life makes.

THE PURPOSE OF LIFE

Spiritual people aren't trying to protect their personalities from life, nor are they trying to feed their egos with the world's goodies. They're not trying to manipulate the people, places, and things around them to build up wealth or power or to protect themselves from the pain and fear that we all experience.

Spiritual people aren't playing the money game, the power game, the security game, the status game, or any other game associated with life's external dimension. They're playing the consciousness game. The object of this game is to use each moment of life as a tool for increasing our self-awareness.

For those who strive for greater consciousness, money is no different from relationships, work, or other parts of our lives in its value as a tool for growing in self-awareness. What's different is how ignorant we are of the possibilities inherent in using money this way.

INTO THE LIGHT: THE PURPOSE OF THIS BOOK

This book can help you free yourself from your deeply ingrained patterns of belief and behavior concerning money. These beliefs may hinder or help you today; the fact that they condition your behavior means you're not as conscious or free as you could be. And whatever limitations you have placed on your consciousness, either knowingly or unknowingly, stand between you and a more personal and direct experience of the Divine Presence.

WHAT'S COMING

Following an introduction to spirituality, the early chapters will sensitize you to your attitudes and beliefs about money. Others will cover the childhood origins of our beliefs, what money means to us, and how these beliefs affect our behavior.

Most chapters contain exercises that can help you learn about your particular money psychology. The more we learn, the more free we can become.

Some chapters will challenge you to list and prioritize your most cherished and deeply held personal values. You'll be asked what you *really* believe in. You'll also be asked to decide what the most meaningful work would be for you and to plot a course in that direction.

Later chapters will show you how to use money as a tool for spiritual growth. They'll discuss spiritual principles that you can use money to experience. You'll be presented with exercises that can lead you toward a more conscious life and toward the God of your understanding.

People sometimes incorrectly view spirituality as impractical and ethereal. Spirituality is extremely practical and, ultimately, the most realistic way of living. It takes us away from the fantasies our egos create to protect ourselves from our pain. In so doing, it moves us toward the reality we blind ourselves to in our ego-based ignorance.

Regardless of your religious tradition or spiritual orientation, the material in these pages can help you move along your path. Don't let the particular words used to present an idea get in the way. Substitute the words of your own understanding for any you find in these pages that don't work for you. This book isn't designed to influence your choice of religion or spiritual path. It's meant to challenge you to walk whatever path you've chosen and to give you tools to help you along.

Introduction

THE POINT OF IT ALL

The point isn't for you to memorize what's in these pages. It's to look deeply at yourself and the ways you deal with money. If we do this with intensity, diligence, and without self-judgment, we can change the level of our inner awareness. We can evolve along the spiritual path that lies right in front of us, right now. It's the only path we can walk if we want true spiritual understanding. The path is . . . *you.*

CHAPTER ONE

FALSE PROFITS: MONEY AND SPIRITUALITY

In God We Trust—All Others Pay Cash
—a common sign at truck stops

THE JOURNEY

Once upon a time, a young woman set out from her home in search of truth. Having decided to learn the proper way to live in the world and at the same time lead a life of the spirit, she journeyed to cities, distant mountain peaks, and hidden monasteries in search of those who could help her with her task. No one could answer her to her satisfaction.

After several years of seeking, the woman heard of a great king who knew all the wisdom of the world. Despite the distance, she set out immediately for his palace, crossing two deserts, three mountain ranges, and four rivers before arriving at the gates of the king's palace.

The king admitted her to his presence as soon as he heard she had arrived. "I'm so glad to find another seeker," he exclaimed. "Let's sit comfortably over here and talk about the Divine." They went into a beautiful room furnished with priceless tapestries and rugs and ornaments of gold and silver. Sitting in a chair arranged perfectly by a servant, the king smoothed his silk robes and began to talk about God.

Rather than being impressed, the seeker felt great doubt. How could this man, who wore silk robes and ate from plates of gold, know anything about how to live spiritually? The other teachers she had visited had warned her about wealth and the traps of the world. Surely this man, with his servants and tapestries, could not satisfy her where all the others had failed.

The king spoke enthusiastically, describing the beauties of the divine realm. He gestured, knocking over an oil lamp and spilling some of the oil. The oil began to burn, and the pillow on which the lamp had been set began to smolder. The seeker noticed it, but the king appeared oblivious. She tried to interrupt his enraptured speech to point out the smoldering cushion, but he imperiously waved her back into her chair. "Not now," he said, "I'm talking about God." And he continued.

Soon the pillow caught fire, which spread to a rug and began to burn slowly toward a wall covered with a priceless tapestry. Again the seeker tried to warn her host, and again he stopped her before she could speak: "Don't interrupt, I'm speaking about God."

Finally, the tapestry caught fire. As the flames rose up the wall, the seeker could not contain herself any longer. Leaping to her feet, she yelled at the king: "The tapestry is burning, it's priceless! Soon your palace, too, will burn down!"

The king waved his hand. The fire disappeared. All was as it had been. The seeker was very confused. There had been no danger after all! This king was more than he seemed! As she sat there feeling very confused, the king spoke gently to her.

"My friend, you are more attached to this worldly wealth than I. That is why I have been entrusted with it, while you have been wandering the world seeking truth."

We don't know what ultimately happened to the young woman. Did she become the king's disciple, or did she refuse the lesson and keep wandering? Teaching stories aren't like sitcoms, coming to a neat conclusion with all the loose ends tied together. They're more open-ended, allowing the reader and the listener to put their own experiences into the story and perhaps change its meaning or learn something new from what seemed familiar.

The balance between spiritual and material life has concerned the human race from the very beginning. It's a struggle that everyone who has ever lived has had to resolve. The answers from the past may not necessarily resolve today's questions, but the knowledge that solutions have been found should serve as comfort for those seeking such a balance.

WHAT IS SPIRITUALITY?

A Hasidic story about the spiritual path goes as follows: Two students of a famous rabbi were arguing about the true path to God. The first said that the path was built on effort. "You must follow the Law with all your energy, pray, pay attention, and live rightly," he said. The second disagreed, saying, "Effort is not the path at all. That way is only based on the ego. The path is to surrender, to let go, and to allow the teaching to live in you. 'Not my will but thine.' "

Just then, the rabbi passed by, and the two decided to ask their teacher to settle things. The teacher listened as the first student praised the path of wholehearted effort and, when asked whether this was the true path, the teacher replied "You're right." The second student became upset and eloquently described the path of surrender. He too asked the rabbi whether this was the true path. "You're right," the rabbi replied.

A third student had been listening. He too approached the rabbi, saying, "Teacher, how can I learn from this? They can't both be right."

"You're right, too," replied the Rabbi.*

---

*Christina Feldman and Jack Kornfield, *Stories of the Spirit, Stories of the Heart* (New York: HarperCollins, 1991), 307.

There is a Sufi story that also deals with the dynamics of spiritual work. Two great masters were discussing the spiritual path. A student approached and asked for instruction. One master turned to her and said, "Knock, and keep knocking. You must knock as hard as you can, and someday the door will open." The other master asked the first, "How long are you going to keep lying to these people? Don't you know that the door is always open?"

FOOL'S GOLD

These two stories offer subtle and loving instruction on the spiritual path. The path, at all times and in all traditions, isn't based on the nature of the goal. It isn't based on the ultimate nature and characteristics of the Absolute. That can only be known by those who experience it directly. The rest is theology, speculation. The path is based on the seeker's inner processes, the ways we keep ourselves from seeing the truth and experiencing the Divine in each moment.

Both stories focus on the students' processes toward experience of the Absolute. In the first story the students are arguing about "the path." They think there's one way everyone must approach the experience of God. Their teacher knows better. He tells each of them the truth but does so by answering a slightly different question. The students argue about whether there's one path for everyone. He tells them that the path each one is on is right for the one following it.

In the second story, two masters have disagreed. One tells a student to keep knocking so that someday the door might open. The other points out that the door to the Divine is always open. Who's right? The second master is speaking more accurately: the door *is* always open. But the first master is the better teacher. He knows that it is the student who must open, not the door. He is not concerned with accurately describing the goal. His concern is effectiveness in teaching.

SPIRITUAL FANTASIES

Another traditional Hasidic story illustrates some of the traps on the path. A rabbi was praying in the synagogue. "I am nothing, I am nothing," he repeated. The cantor entered and heard the rabbi's prayer. He joined in, saying, "I am nothing, I am nothing." A janitor was passing by and heard the two men praying. As he began to sweep the floor, he prayed in a quiet whisper, "I am nothing, I am nothing." Hearing the janitor, the cantor nudged the rabbi. "Look who thinks he's nothing."

This humorous story demonstrates the trap of pride. It shows how even a profoundly spiritual exercise designed to make the practitioner less egotistical can become a source of pride. We may adopt spiritual beliefs to make ourselves feel better. People sometimes structure their lives in a spiritual way because it diverts them from their pain or because it provides entertainment for the ego. The beliefs we hold, the rituals we perform, the way we speak and act—if they function to divert us from the real path, we're actually using spirituality to avoid spiritual growth.

We may discover abilities and powers that we think are spiritual and then use them in ways that strengthen our ego and divert us from closely examining ourselves. Seeing the future, knowing what others are thinking, becoming able to strongly influence others, using other psychic powers such as channeling—all this is what most spiritual traditions have called "magic." It's the "dark side of the force," because trying to control things rather than surrendering personal will to the Divine Presence traps the practitioner in his or her ego.

How many people remember that Frankenstein was the name of the doctor, not the monster? In effect, the doctor became the monster, because he abused his talents. Falling into the trap of pride, he tried to do what only the Absolute had done: create life. In this classic story of morality,

Frankenstein's creation destroyed him. Of course, we all get the point: Dr. Frankenstein destroyed himself through misuse of his gifts.

The *Star Wars* movie series is a more recent morality play. When Luke Skywalker finally confronts the emperor, the emperor invites Luke to kill him. "Strike me down," he hisses. "Your hate is strong. Use it." The emperor is trying to trap Luke into becoming a mere power-seeker. If Luke falls into this trap, he'll be doomed to endless combat, and more important, he'll be unable to experience the unity of the "force." He'll be dominated by the emperor, because the emperor is stronger. That's the emperor's secret: once you give in and play the power game, you're always vulnerable to domination by someone stronger—and there's always someone stronger.

The trap of powers and abilities doesn't always lie in dominating others. It can be more subtle than that, more a function of the seeker's need for affirmation or for proof of progress. A Hindu story describes a young seeker who studied with a great teacher. After a year, he became impatient because he hadn't learned any secrets and didn't have any miraculous powers. One day he heard of another teacher who taught his students to walk on water. He left his teacher and studied with the wonder worker.

It took him five years to reach his goal. One day he saw his original teacher on the other side of the river, getting ready to take the ferry across. As the teacher gave the ferry-man a coin to take him across, the student walked over the water and stepped proudly on the bank in front of his former guide. He waited for the praise he knew would come. His teacher asked, "You studied for five years to avoid spending a little money?"

The student probably hadn't even thought about the

money. He was just showing off for his first teacher. By posing the question as he did, the teacher was trying to help the student realize that he had become sidetracked by his desire for power.

REAL GOLD

Nothing shows up false without the true:
the fool took false coin
hoping it might be gold.
If there were no genuine coin in the world,
how would it be possible to pass fakes?
Unless there is truth,
how could there be lies?
Falsity gets its value from the existence of truth.
Some want the wrong in the hope that it will be right.
—Rumi

Jalalludin Rumi, the thirteenth-century mystic poet and master of the whirling dervishes, once knocked on his Beloved's door. "Who's there?" a great voice rang out. "It's me, Rumi, your lover." The voice responded, "Go away. There's no room in here for two."

Despondent, Rumi left. After years of study he returned, again knocking on his Beloved's door. "Who's there?" came the voice. "It's you," Rumi answered—and the door to his Beloved swung open.

All spirituality is based on unity. In some way, at the deepest level, everything that exists is bound together. Everything is one. There is an aspect of reality that is the same everywhere, and this unifying characteristic of the universe is the foundation on which the enormous diversity of everything else depends. Call it God, Christ, Allah, Higher Power, the Void, Satchitananda, Tao, Self, the Great Spirit—

11

all spiritual paths are its expression and have as their ultimate goal the integration of the individual with the greater unity.

When Moses asked who sent the Ten Commandments, the reply came, "Say unto the Children of Israel, I AM hath sent me unto you" (Exodus 3:14). This is the Divine Presence that exists beyond all names, beyond all concepts, and beyond all experience, that can be contained in and described by the awareness we feel at the level of the individual personality. We are droplets, and the Divine Presence is the ocean. When the drop reaches the ocean, it merges into the greater identity. It's still water, still there, but not in separate form.

The purpose of all spirituality is to transform the seeker so he or she can experience the Divine Unity. This is mysticism, not theology. Mysticism is knowing God directly; theology is knowing about God by having read a lot.

But to know the Absolute directly, you must first know yourself. Mysticism is based on the discovery, in all times and among all peoples, that there are great truths buried inside each of us, and that these are available only to the contemplative spirit.

This book uses the words *God, Divine Presence,* and *Absolute* to refer to this transcendent unity. If they're not satisfactory to you, please substitute the terms of your understanding.

SPIRITUALITY IN THE MATERIAL WORLD

Think of the most spiritual person you can imagine. What image comes to you? Many people think of an ascetic, perhaps a wanderer, wearing a robe, owning nothing.

This archetype of spirituality resonates deeply in us, whether it's a historical figure such as the Buddha or Jesus, a literary character like Siddhartha in the novel by Hermann Hesse, or a television character like Cain in the "Kung Fu" series. It can teach us a great deal about the inner aspects of the spiritual path. Doesn't the Bible say that "it is easier for a camel to go through the eye of a needle, than for a rich man to enter into the kingdom of God"? (Matthew 19:24). Isn't poverty more spiritual than wealth? Shouldn't people with wealth feel guilty?

There's a difference between external poverty and inner, or spiritual, poverty. *Spiritual* poverty refers to an inner state rather than to the amount of wealth we have; it is a spiritual sense of destitution and neediness, of being lost and incomplete.

Most spiritual traditions do warn about the ways that owning things and having material wealth can divert us from the attitude we need to experience unity with the Absolute. But the essential problem isn't owning things, it's in our reaction to owning them. The experience of possessing things and wanting more of them reinforces the sense of self as separate from the rest of existence and leads to efforts to gain more things. We are distracted from the true source of security, power, and existence: the Divine Presence.

Spiritual poverty means being in need of the Absolute and not accepting anything else in its place. It means not allowing ourselves to be diverted by anything else we can have, no matter how attractive it might be on a superficial level. The things of the world can be beautiful and seductive, causing the seeker to forget the ultimate goal: unity with the Absolute.

This is why different traditions speak of "the dark night of the soul" and "being in despair." The world's wonders surround us, and it's so easy to forget our true aim. However, even the attraction we feel to what the world offers us can help us on the path. It's as if we knew of a great storehouse of true wealth but didn't have any of it. Knowing the wealth is there and that it's possible to get to it can fuel much of the spiritual journey.

13

WHAT'S THE REAL THING?

It's easy to confuse false wealth with the real thing. This is one of the great themes running throughout most of the world's religious traditions. False wealth implies independence and self-sufficiency, the capacity to exist without the Divine Presence. This is why the world's religions have tended to view poverty positively and why money and things are seen as traps. The struggle for money and things as ends in themselves confuses false wealth with real wealth, serves as a barrier to inner growth, and is a diversion from the spiritual path.

The ascetic model, that of the person who has renounced the world, can teach us a great deal about the spiritual path. However, the model of the saint also has something to teach us. The saint lives in the world with all the relationships and entanglements everyone has but never forgets God for a single moment. The saint lives in the world but isn't *of* the world.

This spiritual archetype opens a door to spirituality in the material world. It can show us how to enter into the life of the outer world without losing our inner freedom and how to remember the Divine Presence while not allowing our awareness to be captured by anything else.

WE DESERVE A BREAK TODAY

If we can stay focused on our intention to experience the Absolute as we experience each moment of our life, we create a "break" in our awareness. This break is a gap between our awareness of ourselves and our awareness of what we're experiencing. If we can begin to differentiate between us and what happens to us, we have taken an important step on the path.

There's a difference between the experience of "I'm unhappy" and "I'm experiencing unhappiness." If we are our experiences, then they control us. If we have an inner sense of self that is beyond any temporary experience, then we have created an opening into which a new kind of awareness can grow. This new awareness can help us see things more as they are, rather than as how we've allowed ourselves to believe they were. This is the beginning of the path to inner freedom.

THE MORE WE SEE, THE MORE WE CAN BE

The more we see, the more we understand. The more we understand, the less we allow ourselves to be controlled by events and emotions. The less controlled we are by externals, the more free we become. The more free we are, the more we can experience the Divine Presence. Finally, the more we experience the Divine Presence, the more we see. The process is self-perpetuating.

HEAVEN AND HELL

This is what life can be about: using each moment as a way of experiencing the Divine Presence. This approach can guide us to an understanding of heaven and hell. Hell, in functional and spiritual terms, is the state of moving further from an experience of the Divine Presence; Heaven is the state of moving closer to it.

A traditional Zen story illustrates this idea. A great swordsman heard about a Zen master and demanded an audience. "Teach me about heaven and hell," he bellowed as the master sat drinking tea. "You are an ugly fellow," said the master, "and your mother was a whore. You are too stupid to learn from someone as intelligent as I."

The swordsman became enraged. His sword flashed out, and just as it was about to descend, the master said softly, "That's hell." The swordsman froze. He realized that the master had risked his life to help him take a step on the path. He felt awe for the master's selfless commitment to the truth and bowed in gratitude. "That's heaven," said the master.

15

OH, HELL

So there is a hell—right here, right now, right in front of us all the time. And there's also a heaven—in exactly the same place. Whatever moves us toward the Divine Presence is heavenly, and whatever moves us away from it is hellish.

LIVING SPIRITUALLY IN THE MATERIAL WORLD

We can integrate our spiritual beliefs with the way we live by

- living our values
- finding good work
- making our daily lives a tool for self-awareness
- opening ourselves to the Divine Presence

LIVING OUR VALUES

It's important to live in harmony with our most deeply held personal values. Living this way brings harmony to what we do and to our inner life. It also makes us more capable of experiencing the Absolute. Living in conflict with what we believe adds to our inner sense of separation from the Divine Presence. And while the experience of that separation is often a powerful motivating force on the path, the seeker's ultimate goal is always harmony.

If you work through the exercises in the coming chapters, you'll start building a clear understanding of your personal values. These are the principles you care about most, the ones you want to live for.

FINDING GOOD WORK

Work is so important an experience—almost primal in Western, particularly North American, life—that what we do helps define us to ourselves as well as to others.

E. F. Schumacher outlined the three essential purposes of "good work" shown at the top of page 17.

16

1. To provide necessary and useful goods and services.
2. To enable us to use and thereby perfect our gifts and talents like good stewards.
3. To engage in this work in service to and in cooperation with others, which helps liberate us from our inborn egocentricity.*

Having good work implies that we've taken responsibility for our material needs. If we haven't, we'll be caught in a web of dependent behaviors and relationships that can drain our energy and make life more difficult. It's important to be grounded in daily life to provide a base of stability for the great demands spirituality will make. This book contains exercises that will help you start defining what good work might be for you.

MAKING OUR DAILY LIVES A TOOL FOR SELF-AWARENESS

If we know how to live, each moment is like a soft brushing of fine sandpaper over a piece of beautiful but rough wood. Stroke after stroke slowly removes the edges and uneven parts, and the inner beauty of the fine grain gradually becomes visible.

If we know how to live, we can use each moment to grow in self-awareness. We can become more aware of our personal psychology and patterns of behavior. We can become more free of the habits and patterns we've adopted on the basis of that psychology. That is self-refinement, and we can learn how to do it in each moment of our lives, regardless of what we're doing or what's happening to us.

This book contains many different exercises for gaining self-awareness. It will help you learn to use your moment-to-moment experience of life as a tool for self-refinement.

---

*E. F. Schumacher, *Good Work* (New York: Harper & Row, 1979), 3-4.

OPENING OURSELVES TO THE DIVINE PRESENCE

It's as if God were broadcasting on the FM band, and most of us were tuned to AM. The FM stations are "on the air," so anyone with the right receiver can pick them up. But it's hard to do when our equipment isn't tuned properly. We have to change our capacity to receive by switching to the right band, so we can receive those other broadcasts.

Spirituality means learning how to be open to the Divine Presence. There are deliberate steps we can take to increase our capacity to be open. These practices might include prayer, concentration, meditation, chanting, movement, singing, or other technologies the human race has evolved to open the individual to mystical experience. By practicing whatever means we've chosen, we can increase our capacity to receive whatever the Absolute wants to send us.

Spirituality is a process of purification and receptivity. It's a way of life that leads from what we believe through what we do for a living, to how we live in every moment, and, ultimately, to increasing our capacity to receive the Divine Presence.

PENNIES FROM HEAVEN

The Evil One threatens you with poverty,
and bids you to conduct unseemly.
—Qur'an II:268

How many of us have felt fear of not having enough, of not being able to survive, of not having what we want for ourselves and others? This fear leads us to all sorts of behavior that keeps us from an experience of the Absolute. Fear is the problem, not the possibility of poverty.

If real spirituality is based on unity, then any separation in the way we perceive what we're experiencing moves us away from spirituality. As soon as we say, "This is spiritual, but that isn't," we've created a perceptual separation that stops our growth. The separation doesn't really exist in the experiences but in ourselves. If we don't experience something as spiritual, then we've cut ourselves off from our spirituality as long as the experience lasts. If work and money aren't spiritual, how much time are we wasting?

Many people believe that the intellectual and scientific progress of the last century has allowed us to free ourselves of a life dominated by religion and religious institutions. They believe that social, political, and economic progress has freed us from the need for spiritual awareness. Have our wonderful achievements allowed us to sense the Absolute more clearly? Or have they merely confused us and added more veils to our eyes?

In the life of a people there are . . . two halves. One constitutes the play of its earthly existence, the other its relationship with the Absolute. Now what determines the value of a people or of a civilization is not the literal form of its earthly dream—for here everything is only a symbol—but its capacity to "feel" the Absolute.

—Frithjof Schuon

In the long run, it's not our material accomplishments that will determine our contribution to the history of the human race. It will be the extent of our capacity to sense the Divine Presence in the worldly or mundane aspects of our lives that will give our civilization its long-term value in human history.

Jacob Needleman says that our problem with money isn't that we take it too seriously, but rather that we don't take it seriously enough. If we gave it more importance, he suggests, we'd understand it better, we'd put it in its proper place in life, and it would have less power over us. Money's proper place, he concludes, is secondary to our spiritual values.[*]

WHERE DOES SPIRITUALITY BEGIN?

All spiritual traditions agree that the path to experiencing the Absolute begins inside us. "Know thyself," the Greek gnostics said. "The Kingdom of Heaven is within," the Gospels say. The Qur'an says, "Whoever knows himself knows his Lord."

In our society almost everything we do relates to money in some way. Our experience of money—what it means to us, how we feel about it, how we use it, the emotional context within which we make financial decisions—is therefore one of the most powerful tools we have for increasing our self-awareness on a daily basis. The beginning of real spiritual work is to see what we really do, how we act and feel. It's the first step on the path to inner freedom.

THE GAME'S THE SAME

Rabbi Yishmael said: One who wishes to acquire wisdom should study the way that money works, for there is no greater area of Torah-study than this. It is like an everflowing stream.
—Talmud: Bava Batra 175b

Learning to live spiritually means learning to use every aspect of our lives as a way of seeing ourselves more clearly. Suppose we could learn about the way we give and receive love by observing how we give and receive something else. Suppose that other thing is easier to observe than love, because it's more concrete. That would be a powerful tool, wouldn't it?

---

[*]Jacob Needleman, *Money and the Meaning of Life* (New York: Doubleday, 1991).

If you carefully observe yourself and others giving and receiving money, you'll see how emotionally complex the process is. It brings up issues of inferiority and superiority, self-image, social persona, how one deals with power, how one expresses and receives love, and more. And while giving may be blessed, receiving well is much harder.

PRO CHOICE

Jesus said, "Render unto Caesar that which is Caesar's, and unto God that which is God's" (Matthew 22:21). Needleman points out that Jesus doesn't suggest ignoring Caesar. Rather, both obligations receive equal mention, and Caesar is mentioned first. Jesus is telling us that we must first fulfill the obligations of our daily lives and then go on to the spiritual realm.

In today's monetized culture, rendering unto Caesar means understanding how money functions in our inner and outer lives. Money has many associations for us, we give it many different meanings, and it plays an incredibly important role in our lives.

By reading this book and completing the exercises, you'll begin to understand the importance money has for your inner life. Only by giving it this level of attention and awareness can you learn to put money in its proper place in your life. By increasing your awareness of how you experience money, you can also become aware of what's more important than money: your experience of the Divine Presence. It appears paradoxical, but it isn't, really: by taking money more seriously, it becomes of secondary importance to you.

CONCLUSION

Money can serve as a powerful mirror in which we can see ourselves and our behavior very clearly. The meanings we give to money, the behavior we engage in to get it, the ways we use and spend it, and the needs money satisfies are all doors to greater self-awareness and inner freedom. If spiritual growth is based on inner freedom and an enhanced awareness, what serious seeker can afford *not* to use money as a tool for spiritual growth?

CHAPTER TWO

MAKING SENSE OF MONEY

We can use money to live a more spiritual life. We don't need a lot of money to do this. We don't have to buy anything in particular, travel anywhere, or even give money to worthy causes. This book will show you how to use the ways you think, feel, and behave around money as tools for personal and spiritual growth.

Does dealing with money make you feel anxious? Dumb? Inadequate? Insecure? Out of control? Do you want more of it? Are you embarrassed by how much you have? Do you have difficulty spending on yourself or others? Do you spend impulsively or compulsively? Do you think that money measures success? Do you have contempt for money? Do—or did—you and your partner fight about it? Are you repeating your parents' patterns with money or rebelling against them?

Is your life with money—your daily life earning it, spending it, saving it, and relating to how others use it—out of sync with your most deeply held personal values? Do you feel a gap between who you are in your heart and how you act in the world?

LET'S MAKE SENSE

War begetteth poverty; poverty, peace.
Peace maketh riches flourish; wonders never cease.
Riches beget pride; pride is war's best ground.
War begetteth poverty; the world goeth round.
—English Round

How can we make sense of money? It affects us so deeply and in so many ways. Money is involved in almost everything we do, from providing ourselves with the necessities of life to the recreation we choose for our leisure hours to our most intimate relationships.

How much of your time is spent in earning and using money? How many times a day do you see money change hands? How many times a day do you consider purchasing something or look at the price of something? How many advertisements do you see in a day? Each time you come in contact with or consider using money, you activate your entire money psychology.

Financial decisions often seem difficult because we make them within an extremely complex and unconscious emotional framework. Whenever you use money or consider a financial issue, your particular set of emotional patterns is activated. This set of patterns then guides you in your behavior. It also predisposes you toward certain kinds of answers to financial questions.

Most of the time we're not aware that this is happening. We may think that money is an incredibly difficult aspect of life and that we're just not very competent when dealing with it. We're like puppets, unaware of the strings that make us dance. And because we remain unaware of our emotional patterns regarding money, we keep looking toward money as the solution to our problems.

SURROUNDED BY MONEY

Money is like air. It's around us all the time, but we're rarely conscious of it. We're usually as unaware of our psychological relationship with money as we are of the pressure of the air on our skin.

You'd think that anything that occupied and mystified us to such an extent would be a constant topic of conversation and a target for deep, ongoing analysis of our relationship with it. Exactly the opposite is the case. Most of the time we deal with our relationship with money by avoiding thinking or talking about it.

WHAT IS MONEY?

Money is one of the most important social inventions in history. It ranks with language, fire, and the wheel in the extent to which it has changed every aspect of human life. And our particular society and culture, to an extent unmatched by previous ones, are structured around earning and spending money.

Economists will tell you that money is a medium of exchange and a store of value. They mean that money gives us a measuring tool to compare the value of different things so we don't have to constantly barter for them. Money also allows us to accumulate purchasing power for the future. This is trying to define money by what it *does*. It really doesn't get at what money *is*.

IT'S ALL IN YOUR MIND

Money can take the physical form of metal coins, paper notes, plastic cards, and printed numbers on a page. Stones, shells, tobacco, cattle, people, cigarettes, animal skins, and many more things have also served as money. Despite money's wide variety of physical manifestations, however, it's ultimately a mass psychological agreement. When everyone agrees that something is money, regardless of its physical form, that thing becomes money. Take the physical form elsewhere, where people aren't part of the agreement, and its function as money disappears.

Value is a psychological phenomenon, and for something to be a measurement of it, everyone has to agree on that measure. Money is like an inch, a foot, a yard, or a meter: these are arbitrary measurements we have agreed on over time.

The first monies came from things that were needed in daily life but were rare. Over time, the use of money became better organized and its manifestations more abstract. People became more accustomed to money, and accepted the concept more readily. Rulers began identifying themselves with this wonderful invention by controlling what could be used as money and by putting their likenesses on it.

For many centuries, gold and silver were the most important forms of money. The psychological agreement on their value stemmed from their relative scarcity and their uses as ornamental jewelry and signs of royalty.

The demands of international trade and the cleverness of merchants and bankers resulted in the development of paper money. This money had no intrinsic value and wasn't scarce. It was "backed" by something else: a trader's honesty and a banker's willingness to convert the paper into something that was more generally agreed to be valuable.

As the centuries passed, the needs of trade and the sophistication of society increased. Today we have left behind the necessity to back our currency with something that's allegedly more valuable. Our faith in our country ultimately backs our money.

Take a banknote from your wallet. How do you know it's money? That's easy—you recognize it as such. You learned to identify it as money at an early age. Everyone around you identified it as money, so you did too. You can prove it's money by spending it: if others accept it, it's money.

It's everyone's acceptance of something that makes it a medium of exchange. That acceptance is a psychological attitude. When people come to believe that everyone else will accept something as money, they're willing to use it themselves. You can hear echoes of this in credit card commercials: "Our card is accepted in 457,600 places around the globe. . . ." The underlying argument is that if so many places accept this card, you should run out and get one. This acceptance is a psychological event: the public adopts a belief in something's usefulness as a medium of exchange.

Once you understand that money is a psychological as well as a physical phenomenon, you can begin to see how complex our relationship with it is. Learning about money is not just a matter of learning the techniques of sound money management. If that were so, then the thousands of books that have been published on this topic would have helped the millions of people who have read them feel more comfortable with money.

Since that's not the case, since the most common cause of divorce is arguments over money, since most people report having major problems with money, and since most of us are completely unaware of how deeply money affects us, there must be a better way to begin dealing with the problem of money.

THE LAST TABOO

We've reacted to all of this by making the psychology of money a taboo subject. Just as sex was a forbidden subject for public discussion until fairly recently, the subject of money remains taboo also. People may share their frustrations about not having enough of it but never the details of their finances, their behavioral problems with money, or how it makes them feel.

Movie stars will write books that describe their sexual encounters and will discuss their problems on national television shows. They don't write books describing how much money they make, their problems with it, and how money makes them feel. That's too personal.

People are used to talking about their sex lives. If you

want to really offend others, ask how much they make and how much they spend on various things. That's really intrusive. Money is the last taboo.

THE AFFLICTION OF MONEY

Part of our fascination with movie stars, rock musicians, and athletes is based on our knowledge that they earn huge amounts of money. Watching people deal with a sudden superabundance of money can be very instructive.

Sudden wealth is a very difficult situation to handle. It can be overwhelming. Sudden wealth often leads people who are unprepared and perhaps relatively uneducated and quite young to excessive and self-destructive behavior. It pulls them off balance and distorts their self-image and social persona.

We see in these situations exaggerated versions of what happens to the rest of us as we deal with money. The attitudes, beliefs, and behavior may be more subtle, but they're not less important.

Money can afflict us because it can lead us to live in a fantasy world. We live not in the present moment, but in a world of yearning and envy. And often what we crave isn't what we would choose for ourselves. We want it as the result of what we've learned gradually and unconsciously over our lives.

FOOL'S GOLD: FALSE WEALTH

Gwen was a successful solicitor at a large firm in Washington, D.C. Her annual income ran into six figures— not bad for a forty-year-old. Her eighty-hour work week dominated her life, and her social life necessarily revolved around her work. Gwen loved the fast pace, the challenge, and the money. Then she quit.

"I went through a real emotional crisis," she says. "I liked the pace, the challenge, but it all felt wrong for me. I was out of balance. My health wasn't good, my emotional life was nonexistent, and I was wearing myself out. There was nothing wrong with what I was doing, but it wasn't me."

Gwen is still a solicitor—at a small firm in a city in the

Southwest. Her income is less than one sixth of what it was—but her personal satisfaction is much greater. "Now my values and my life are in sync," she says. She has become more active in her religious life as well. With a less fast-paced life, she has begun reading contemplative literature and is looking for a church to join.

Many people are chasing false wealth in their lives. What they are after wouldn't satisfy them if they had it. Their lives are out of sync with what they really believe in. What they do doesn't flow from cherished and deeply held personal values. They're doing what they think they should do, or what they think they have to do, or they're just doing, without much thought. They're trapped.

Real wealth, in financial terms, is having enough and being content. Going beyond the financial realm, real wealth means living a life in sync with your personal values. This results in a sense of "wellth," which is the real reward we can have in our life.

When our lives are in harmony with our values, they seem to flow from inside us rather than being imposed on us from outside. We don't have to hide parts of ourselves to protect them. We're nourished on all levels by our daily life. Our life and who we are are the same.

In addition, real wealth involves a sense of spirituality, a relationship with the Absolute. We're really wealthy when our sense of spirituality becomes the context within which we do everything else.

BLINDED BY IDOLATRY

Confusing worldly things, including money, with the Absolute is idolatry. Idolatry is a sin, not for moral reasons and not because it offends a vengeful God, but because it confuses us and prevents us from coming into contact with the Divine Presence within us. It focuses our attention outside when in reality, as St. Francis of Assisi said, "What you are looking for is what is looking."

> *Who will prefer the jingle of jade pendants*
> *when he once has heard stone growing in cliff?*
> —Lao Tzu

Has our confusion of false wealth with real wealth doomed us? Many people feel that way. They think our entire society and way of life are rotten and senseless. They think everything has to change before anything can get better. Many people who call themselves spiritual feel this way. They feel profoundly alienated from contemporary life and often idealize life in other cultures or simpler ways of life that they believe existed in the past.

This pessimism can be a subtle form of idolatry and a great rationale for procrastination; it becomes idolatry when it makes social conditions a barrier between human beings and the Absolute. This shouldn't be, of course. If the Divine Presence is everywhere and has always been everywhere, then social conditions cannot come between the seeker and the path.

Rejecting society can lead people to procrastinate because if everything has to change before anything can get better, there's nothing an individual can do until then. Why take any small action, if it will make no difference in that vast scale of change that has to happen?

During the Cold War, many people were curiously accepting of, and sometimes almost hopeful about, the possibility of Armageddon. Perhaps they hoped that a nuclear war would cleanse us of our inner deficiencies. This view, however, was a projection of their need to confirm their negative image of society and themselves. They ignored the wonderful and positive aspects of themselves, our society, and our way of life.

These are just a few of our positive aspects as a society: We often bring a wonderful intensity and sincerity to our efforts. We honor single-minded dedication. We read books and take courses in time management to learn to be more productive. We study the qualities of success with a rare single-mindedness. These qualities themselves are part of our national wealth.

Spiritual people who haven't learned how to be effective in the world may have further to go on the path than effective people who haven't yet discovered their spirituality. It's harder to change ourselves than it is to see something new: we can see the truth in an instant, but it takes time and effort to learn the skills of effective people.

THE GOLDEN PATH: FROM FOOL'S GOLD TO THE REAL THING

The journey from fool's gold to the real thing starts with belief in the Divine Presence and proceeds through intense self-awareness of our relationship with the wealth of this world. Since we have made money the archetype of wealth, our relationship with money can become a powerful part of our spiritual work, of our search for genuine contact with the Absolute.

The journey isn't easy. You'll have to give intense attention to what you do and how you feel about it. You'll have to observe yourself honestly and without judgment or self-deception. This is difficult and demanding work. There's only this to commend it: it produces results.

The material and exercises in this book can help you. You may have to do some of them over and over; others may work immediately. Your path may also require therapy, participation in a support group or Twelve Step program, further reading, meditation, prayer, engaging the services of a financial adviser, or something else altogether. You'll become the teacher you need!

When we understand more about ourselves, we gain "insight," that is, we see more deeply into what things mean. As we gain insight, the way we see things—our "outlook"—changes. Although we often think the world has changed, it's really we who have become different.

That's why real wealth isn't "out there." Real wealth is inside us. Remember—this doesn't mean that the things of the world aren't important. They are. It means that we have the capacity to put them in their proper place: second in importance to our relationship with the Divine Presence.

CHAPTER THREE

YOUR MONEY AUTOBIOGRAPHY

Even as children, we knew a lot about money. We knew what money meant to our parents, and we agreed or disagreed with them. We knew that money was important. We knew money could buy nice things. We knew that people worked for money. We knew money could be used to reward or punish.

OPENING THE DOOR

The first step to understanding our behavior with money is to see where the behavior came from. When we understand how we learned our attitudes and beliefs about money, and why we behave as we do, we have an opportunity to begin changing behavior that doesn't work for us.

Sam remembers: "Every time Uncle Julius came over, he'd take the change from his pockets and toss it on the floor for the children to scramble after. He enjoyed it, and so did we—it was the game, not the money, really. My parents always got angry, though, and I stopped enjoying it. I've been a little uncomfortable with money ever since. It makes me feel childish."

Sam hates making financial decisions. He chose a career as a social worker, in part so he wouldn't have to work with money. He married an accountant, and she manages their money. He's always been contemptuous of people who work primarily for money.

Sam's wife began to resent having complete responsibility for their finances. They began to argue about money, which was exactly what Sam had been trying to avoid. Although he first blamed his wife for the arguments, Sam gradually came to see that it was really his behavior and attitudes, the result of his childhood experiences, that caused the problem he faced. He saw how they guided and limited his life. Sam has started therapy to work through his relationship with money and is keeping a journal of his thoughts and behavior. "This is a great opportunity to grow," he says.

Many of our childhood attitudes and beliefs about money stay with us through our entire lives. They are the foundation of our current behavior with money. These attitudes and beliefs affect the way we behave in other parts of our lives as well.

We shouldn't be surprised. After all, we look to our childhood for the origins of other aspects of our behavior. Most psychological issues are rooted in our childhood experience. Our self-image, our social persona, our choice of career, our attitude toward success, our feelings about having power, our patterns in intimate relationships, and a great deal more are intertwined with our attitudes and beliefs about money.

CHILDHOOD AGREEMENTS

Roberta's parents always worried about money. They always felt threatened, regardless of how much money they had, and they argued constantly about various expenditures. Each toy or new item of clothing was purchased grudgingly. Each expenditure seemed to threaten the entire family.

Roberta vowed that she'd have enough money when she grew up. She'd learned that money was scarce and that security comes from having enough of it. She divorced her first husband because he didn't feel the same way about money. Her second husband shares her feelings. They're spending as little as possible on themselves and saving everything they can.

Children make agreements with money. Each agreement starts as a belief about money or a meaning the child agrees to give to money. Children are wonderful observers, and they see people around them—parents and other adults, siblings, friends, and people on television—using money and being affected by it. They see what money means to others and how money makes them act and feel.

As children integrate what they see into their own psychology and behavior, each new belief or meaning is layered on top of the old ones. The beliefs and meanings then become self-confirming and shape the child's perceptions and feelings. Like adults, children tend to shape their perceptions according to what they already believe.

Each belief about money, each meaning we give it, is an agreement to feel a certain way when dealing with it. If we begin believing that money means love, then the more money that is spent on us, the more loved we'll feel. If we believe that money is the source of security, we'll feel more secure when we have more, and insecure if we try to spend "too much."

Some agreements are negative. Children see a parent or someone else behaving in a way they don't like, and they swear not to be like that. Perhaps a parent uses money to dominate others, or as a substitute for love, or to punish. Children often swear not to emulate people who've affected them deeply in a negative way. They're as dominated by a negative agreement as by any other kind.

People often say that money makes them feel dumb, or anxious, or insecure. They're really saying they've agreed to believe certain things about money and about themselves in relation to money.

THE FIRST STEP

As we become aware of when and how our beliefs and attitudes about money began, we take the first step toward changing them. As we see the meanings we've learned to give to money and the ways we've agreed to let money make us feel, we'll begin to see how money has affected our behavior in other parts of our lives.

This insight can create an inner space that will let us begin to free ourselves of these patterns of feeling, thought, and behavior. We'll then be able to substitute beliefs and attitudes that serve us in more positive ways.

EXERCISE: SELF-ASSESSMENT

The following questions are designed to help you remember when and how you began learning about money. Their purpose is to sensitize you to the origins of your issues with money; you'll move on to the present day in the chapters that follow. Try to focus entirely on your childhood as you consider these questions.

Don't rush through them. Sit with each one for a while, and let your mind roam back into your childhood. Write down whatever answers come to you; there may be patterns or connections you don't see at first. Even if a question doesn't apply to your family, write down why.

Don't get caught up in your reactions to what you remember. Try to be a neutral observer. It's particularly important to avoid judging yourself, either positively or negatively. Most people find it very helpful to write their answers and reactions to the various exercises in a journal or notebook.

1. In general terms, what do you remember about money from your childhood? What specific events come to mind?

Do you remember having strong feelings about money or others' behavior with it?

2. What specific beliefs about money do you remember learning in childhood? Examples might include

- Money can't buy happiness or love.
- Everyone has a price.
- Money is the root of all evil.
- Money is the most important thing in the world.
- Nice people don't talk about money.
- Money doesn't grow on trees.

3. What do you remember about how your mother, father, or other adults who raised you felt about money? How did they behave with money? Did they fight or argue about money, either actively or passively? How did they use money in their relationships with you and others around them? Did you want to be like them, or did you vow you'd be different?

4. Did you receive an allowance? Did you have to work for it? Did you have to account for what you did with it? Was withholding it used to punish you?

5. Were your brothers and sisters treated any differently than you were? If so, how? Was this a source of strife between you and your siblings?

6. How did your peers' attitudes and behavior affect yours? Was their behavior similar or different? Was your economic status the same, higher, or lower than theirs? Were you under pressure to wear certain clothes, have certain things, or spend money certain ways? Did you feel envy, resent-

ment, superiority, guilt, or shame?

7. Did your religious upbringing, if any, affect your attitude toward money? How?

8. Are there any other events or aspects of your childhood that affected your attitudes toward money or how you behave with it? These might include inheritances, bankruptcies, being on welfare, suddenly having a lot of money, or losing a lot of money.

GREAT EXPECTATIONS

You may have remembered quite a bit as you considered these questions. You may have remembered patterns of belief and behavior exhibited by your parents and others around you. You may also have recalled your childhood emotions about all this.

Although you may have had some powerful insights, don't expect your life to change immediately. Your goal for now is simply to become more aware of how you began learning about money. The next chapter will help you analyze your current beliefs and behavior patterns.

It takes time for understanding to penetrate the behavior patterns you've built up over a lifetime. It takes energy and determination to stay focused on these issues and find ways you'd rather feel and behave to put in place of the old patterns.

The insights you've had are the first step on the path to change. They may be pleasant or unpleasant, but you should feel good about having them. They're the first results of your efforts to change.

THE COURAGE TO CHANGE

As you start to see the origins of your beliefs and attitudes about money, and how they've come to affect your life, it will be tempting to shut the process off. You might not like what you see. You might feel intimidated by how deeply and how long you've been involved in such self-defeating patterns of emotion and behavior. You might feel angry, afraid, or ashamed.

If those feelings arise, observe them as you observed your memories. Don't try to deny them, and don't do whatever you usually do to avoid feeling them.

It's particularly important not to feed them more energy. Don't be angry about being angry, ashamed of feeling ashamed, and so on. Doing that locks you more deeply into these patterns. The fear, anxiety, shame, and similar feelings are proof that your efforts are bearing fruit. They're part of the next step.

BECOME A SPACE EXPLORER

The more you observe all this, the more you'll start to experience a space between your old patterns and your reactions. This space is a gap in time between the stimulus to a certain behavior and the behavior itself. It is the "break," or increased self-awareness, discussed in chapter 1, and it can be a door for a new energy to enter your life.

You'll have a chance, a small one at first, to not feel or behave in the old way. In the beginning, the space will come and go so quickly that you won't be able to take advantage of the opportunity. However, over time you'll become more aware of these opportunities. You won't take the stimuli that used to lead to certain reactions as personally as you did before.

As you become less and less emotionally involved in reacting to the things that used to disturb you, you'll develop a new presence. This presence of mind is what many spiritual traditions call "mindfulness," and it's a major step forward on the path.

We're creatures of habit; we learn by repetition. Our responses are patterns we learn by repetition. We may have to deal with the same feeling or behavior over and over again. This can be very depressing—"Oh, no, not again! Didn't I deal with this already?"

The process isn't a straight line. It's like an upward spiral. We move up along the spiral, circling the same complex set of emotions and behavior patterns, coming back to the same ones over and over. Each time, however, we're coming from a slightly more elevated point of view. Each time we confront ourselves, the act itself is proof that we're progressing.

THE PATH OF INTENSITY

A man heard about a wise woman who lived far away. He traveled a long time and finally found her house. He knocked, entered, and was taken to her. "I've heard you are very wise," he told her, "and I wish to learn your wisdom. Can you sum it up for me?" She looked at him with great love and wrote one word on a piece of paper. She handed it to him. He looked at it. She had written "Attention!"

"Is this all?" the seeker cried. "I've traveled so far, and all you have is one word?" The teacher looked at him again and took out another piece of paper. Again she wrote something down and handed it to him. The seeker read it eagerly. "Attention! Attention!" it said.

Now the man became angry. "You're nothing but a fraud!" he yelled. "How could this be the sum of your wisdom? There must be more than that! I have to know the truth!" With a searching look at him, the teacher wrote three words on another piece of paper: "Attention! Attention! Attention!"

The seeker left the wise woman's house, thinking deeply about what she had said. Lost in thought, he failed to see a cliff in front of him and fell over it. As he fell, however, he grabbed a vine that grew from the rock. Hanging there, his previous concerns forgotten, he noticed some berries growing from a nearby bush. By straining with his free hand, he could just reach far enough to grasp a handful of them. How wonderful they tasted!

This traditional Zen story helps us see that real learning takes place in every instant. The seeker's primary goal is to learn to pay attention to what's happening right now. This is incredibly difficult, because we usually have an internal dialogue of beliefs, attitudes, and thoughts that interprets each moment according to our likes and dislikes.

Paying attention to what's happening, and seeing the difference between what is and our internal dialogue about it, is the first step on the path.

The man in this story expected the wise woman to tell him something he could add to his internal dialogue about life. Since she was really wise, she didn't. She challenged him to give up that dialogue and move into the real world.

This story also describes the intensity of awareness you can bring to each moment. The seeker is experiencing the state of intense attention the wise woman alerted him to. However, it took a threat to his life to get him to that awareness.

It's not necessary to risk our lives to feel more aware. The emotional intensity of our childhood relationship with money can be the fuel for our intense awareness of what's happening now. The more the relationship affected us, the more it hurt us, the more we'll care about changing. This work demands courage, energy, and self-discipline. We have to *care*.

Remember Sam's story at the beginning of the chapter? His desire to stop making himself feel childish, and to stop limiting his life, is the fuel for his growing awareness of how these processes have worked. The more aware he becomes, the more free he'll get.

This is the beauty of the process. It's up to us, right here and now. We can use the emotional intensity of our reactions as a source of energy to do the work. The more personal we make it, the more personally we'll take it. We don't have to go anyplace different or do anything special. All we have to do is live our lives—and pay attention!

CHAPTER FOUR

MONEY MYTHS AND MEANINGS

Wine maketh merry, but money answereth all things.
—Ecclesiastes 10:19

Steve and Katherine fell deeply in love despite their different backgrounds. Steve's family was working-class, and Steve had never had much money, although he hadn't been poor. Katherine's family was wealthy, and she'd never had to work hard for anything.

The couple often fought about money. Steve felt Katherine wasn't part of the real world. When she spent her money on herself or on him, Steve felt threatened, even though he knew she could afford it. He took it personally, too, wondering why she deliberately kept making him feel insecure and dependent.

Katherine felt she'd discovered a new side to Steve. Where was the loving man she'd married? When Steve criticized her spending, he seemed miserly and controlling. She felt he was trying to make her dependent on him. She felt childish whenever they fought and hated herself for feeling that way.

Eventually, Katherine and Steve divorced. To this day, they each believe the other one tried to use money to control his or her partner.

Katherine and Steve weren't really fighting about money.

Their different psychological and emotional patterns with money interacted in ways that threatened them. If they could have risen above the financial issues and dealt with the emotional context of their relationships with money, they would have had a chance to save their marriage.

THE AGONY OF SELF-DEFEATING BEHAVIOR

Bruce grew up poor and was very bitter about it. Highly motivated and very intelligent, he swore he'd always have a lot of money so his family would never suffer what he'd gone through. He worked long hours and bought his wife and children everything he could think of. Bruce couldn't understand why they gradually became alienated from him. He loved them so much!

Bruce's behavior was self-defeating. The very things he did out of love for his family drove them away. They wanted *him*—his time, his love. He devoted his time to work so he could give them things they didn't particularly want. That was how he expressed his love. The harder he tried, the worse things got.

Bruce first blamed himself for not doing enough and then blamed his family for being ungrateful. He cut his children out of his will, and he almost never spoke with them. Bruce's second wife finally got him to discuss his feelings with a family counselor. Over time he understood his children's feelings. He has opened a dialogue with them, and they spend time together regularly.

This story illustrates one of many ways in which the way we act can have exactly the opposite effect of what we intended. Yet, because we adopt behavior based on our previous experiences rather than on the impact of what we're doing, we often go on this way for years or even a lifetime. We may be confused or angry about the gap between our expectations and the way things work out. It often takes a shock, or someone's loving intervention, to help us see that the problem is ours and not the outside world's.

STICKS, STONES, AND BELIEFS ABOUT MONEY

When we say, "Money makes me feel . . . ," we're really describing our personal money psychology. Money can only make us feel a certain way if we believe certain things about it. Our relationship with money, like all other relationships, is inside us, not "out there."

Because people don't understand the dynamics of their relationship with money, they often believe fixing things "out there" would solve their problems. The following common beliefs about money often have destructive and self-defeating consequences:

- Having more money would solve all my problems.
- Money is evil, and the world is evil because it focuses on money so much.
- Controlling my spending limits my freedom and cuts down my enjoyment of life.
- Money is a mysterious force and too difficult for me to understand.
- "They" or "_____" (fill in the group or situation of your choice) keep(s) me from getting ahead.
- Things never go right for me. My investments always go down.
- The amount of money I have is an important measure of my self-worth.
- I express my social persona with money and judge others that way.
- My financial situation is determined by forces outside my control.

All these beliefs are inaccurate or can be *made* inaccurate. They warp our thinking and prevent us from making the most of the money we have and our capacity to earn more of it.

DO YOU KNOW ME?

Here are some common money situations that people get stuck in. Are any of them familiar to you?

Marilyn has worked for her employer for ten years without asking for a raise. She knows others are paid more for the same work she does and watches uncomprehendingly while less competent people are promoted over her head. Although she has grown bitter, she has never complained.

Marilyn's neighbor Anna is fond of saying that money doesn't matter. She contemptuously dismisses people who focus their lives on making money. However, she is often depressed about not having enough money.

George devotes all his time to making money. He knows money isn't what he really wants out of life, but he has fallen into such a good job! He knows he's off the track, but he gets up each day and goes to the office. His blood pressure is high, and he has hired an expensive private trainer who helps him exercise to compensate for what he's doing to his body.

Andy thinks he's a brilliant investor. He constantly finds the most speculative opportunities and is always taking unnecessary financial risks. He thinks making money is a crap game, and you just have to keep rolling the dice until you win the big one. As a result, he is often on the edge of bankruptcy.

Louise refuses to make financial preparations for the future. She thinks society is falling apart and that the world in general is getting worse and worse. "Who knows whether I'll live long enough to retire?" she says. "You've got to live for today." She believes every book she reads that predicts financial, ecological, or political disaster for the human race.

Barbara and Allan have been married for twelve years. Barbara hates dealing with money. She is glad to let Allan handle the family finances, despite his complete financial incompetence. Even though he's lost their life savings, Barbara would still rather let him handle their financial affairs.

David knows exactly what he wants to do with his life: he would like to take some time off and travel around the world. He has had this dream for ten years but keeps putting it off until "someday when I have enough money."

Peter overspends constantly and has built up a dangerously high level of credit card debt. He knows he is in trouble but would rather keep up his life-style than cut back. He is now borrowing from one card to pay the others and soon won't be able to make the full payments at all.

Susan thinks she is conservative and prudent about money. She is a good saver and watches her money like a hawk. Susan is so afraid of losing money, however, that she only invests in the most conservative, lowest-return investments, even for her retirement and other long-term needs.

All these people have inappropriate and self-defeating beliefs about money. Although the beliefs are logical within the framework of each individual's personal psychology, they function destructively in the financial sense. The solutions to their problems don't require more—or less—money. They require changes in the way the individuals think.

THE NEXT STEP: SELF-AWARENESS

By beginning to understand what you learned about money in childhood, you've taken the first step to awareness of your beliefs and attitudes toward money. The exercises that follow will continue this process. They'll sensitize you to the complex emotional context within which you make financial decisions.

1. Did you adopt any of the following beliefs about money in childhood? Write down each one you believed and how you came to think that way. Did your parents or other adults tell you these things? Did you learn from watching their behavior? Did certain events contribute to your beliefs? Are there other beliefs you learned that aren't on this list? Write your answers in as much detail as possible, since the act of writing often draws more information from your memory.

Money is

- an acceptable motivating force
- an unacceptable motivating force
- the root of all evil
- necessary for a happy life
- a way people control and repress others
- a way to get others' respect
- a way to feel good about yourself
- a way to buy freedom and independence
- a source of guilt
- a source of pride
- something you always have to work hard for
- something there's always enough of
- not important at all
- a way to find security
- a way to have fun

Write down any other beliefs you have or have had about money.

2. Use all your senses to make the following situations as

vivid as possible. What would you see, hear, feel, smell, and taste? What would you be thinking? Feeling? Imagine yourself

- asking your boss for a raise
- receiving a large bonus, with all your co-workers watching
- telling a friend you're broke and asking for a loan
- being homeless and asking passers-by for spare change
- trying to collect money from a friend who's "forgotten" the loan
- paying bills, knowing you don't have enough to pay them all
- paying all your bills, knowing you have enough left over for your other needs
- writing a check to your retirement savings plan
- spending a month's income on something you like but don't really need
- figuring out with your spouse where all the money went last month
- winning a large sum in a lottery
- reaching retirement without enough money
- reaching retirement and realizing you're financially independent for the rest of your life

As you put yourself in these situations, you'll activate your money psychology. Your deeper feelings won't spring immediately into awareness, of course. They've been mostly unconscious all your life. But by imagining yourself in these situations, you're creating an inner space for conscious awareness of your feelings and beliefs.

3. What do you like about how you experience and handle money? What don't you like? What is it about each thing that makes you like it or dislike it? Write down as many entries as possible in each category. Examples might include

- I save regularly for retirement.
- I have enough money to pay my bills.
- I live within my means.
- I help others when they're needy.
- I never have money left over for savings.
- I have to borrow regularly to support my life-style.
- I spend impulsively and/or compulsively.
- I do/don't understand investments.
- I enjoy buying things for myself.
- I can't spend on myself.
- I don't spend on anything if I can avoid it.
- I argue with my spouse or partner about money.

This list is certainly not complete! Think about all the things you do with money, and you'll probably find more to add to your list. Don't worry about whether something seems unimportant. (One man doing this exercise liked the way he organized the money in his wallet.)

Again, the key to this exercise is to fully imagine yourself doing each thing you think of. Use your senses. Feel, hear, see, smell, touch. Give yourself time in each situation. Find out what it is about each thing that you like or dislike.

4. Complete the following statement: "Money makes me feel . . ." Don't worry if some of your feelings conflict with others. It's important to do this exercise in a nonjudgmental way. Try to simply observe and write down your feelings and

reactions. If you react strongly to one of your feelings, such as being ashamed about feeling out of control, write that down, too.

5. Look at your answers to exercises 3 and 4. What money behavior would you like to change? What feelings about money would you like to change? Why? What behaviors and feelings do you want to keep? Why?

6. Start keeping a money journal. Carry a small notebook with you throughout the day, and write down any feelings you experience as you confront the use or experience of money. Pay particular attention to your feelings about what you do to make money, the amount you make, how you spend and on what, and on how money affects your closest relationships.

Your feelings may not be immediately obvious. You might find that they're like musical chords, composed of several notes heard together. These "feeling tones" might be crashingly loud or distant and subtle. As you continue working on your journal, your sense of purpose and the act of writing down what you start to remember will focus your awareness and draw forth more and more memories and information. It's like a wake-up call to your subconscious.

Vicky had been keeping her money journal for a month. She was in a department store looking at a dress when she heard her father's voice, saying, "Do you think money grows on trees?"

"It was so real that I spun around to look for him," she wrote later. "For a moment I forgot that he had died three years ago."

That evening, as Vicky considered what had happened,

she became aware of a string of memories about her father and his behavior with money that she'd completely forgotten. He had been a young adult during the Great Depression, and he saved everything, even the envelopes letters came in. He could spend on others and give money to charity, but he never seemed to spend money on himself, even for little things.

Vicky learned a lot about her money background from that one realization. Her father's searing experience in the Depression had been passed to her in an unintended way. She had come to believe that she didn't deserve anything she bought for herself. Now she has the opportunity to let go of that belief.

FEELING FLUSHED

When you've completed these exercises, you'll be much more in touch with your feelings and attitudes about money and your behavior patterns with it.

Remember that you're not doing this to find out that you are a rotten person or to make the burden of your problems a heavier one. Your purpose is to introduce some emotional, behavioral, and spiritual drain-cleaner into your system, to flush out the obstructions that have been clogging up your life.

When you've done this, you'll have created room for healthier patterns to emerge. You'll be able to choose your behavior rather than letting it drive you. You'll be living a more conscious life.

STEP UP ON THE SCALES: THE MEANING OF MONEY

Now we can go on to isolate the meanings you've given to money. While some of what follows might overlap with what you've done before, it really builds on the earlier exercises to give you more information about your money patterns.

Some books categorize people into money "types." More often, however, people find they're a combination of the types or that they behave differently at different times. For this reason, the following exercises give you five emotional scales you can use to help you understand the meanings you've given to money. The five scales are

- importance
- comfort
- dependence
- security
- existence

Our relationships with money are so complex that some of the scales overlap, and all are interrelated. Remember, we're not trying to find a neat category to fit into or a word to describe ourselves. We're just trying to understand.

Each meaning we've given to money is a way we've agreed to let money make us feel. By coming to a greater awareness of these feelings, we have the chance to discard the ones that don't serve us anymore and keep the ones that do.

As you consider each scale, put yourself on a continuum between the extremes. You might find that you feel differently at different times. If so, which feelings are stronger or occur most frequently? You're looking for the dominant themes in your feelings and behavior.

HOW IMPORTANT IS MONEY TO YOU?

Not Important   Very Important
5—4—3—2—1—0—1—2—3—4—5

The first scale is a range from "Money is not important to me at all" at one end to "Money is very important to me" on the other. Importance doesn't necessarily imply a positive experience; money can be very important to us and, at the same time, be a source of profound discomfort.

One of the great myths about money is that having it is necessary for happiness, pleasure, or contentment. "If I just had more money, everything would be great" and "Until I have more money, things can't improve" are versions of this myth.

People often look to the amount of money they have as a measure of their happiness and sense of self-worth and then undermine their happiness by envying or giving exaggerated respect to those who have more than they do. Similarly, their happiness may depend on feeling sorry for or contemptuous of those with less money.

Gordon started his own company and quickly became a millionaire. He believed that he was successful because he was smarter and more deserving than other people. He began ordering his staff around, rather than working *with* them, as he had when he started the company.

He slept with woman after woman who sought to bask in the glow of his success. Gordon never stayed with these dependent women, because his contempt for them kept him from building real relationships. His wife ultimately left him, and he was left with only his sycophantic corporate employees and his latest mistress. Now Gordon has started therapy and is going to men's workshops, trying to discover why he feels hollow and empty.

Gordon hasn't understood yet that he's tried to fill himself up with things that aren't real and don't last. Money was his source of happiness, security, and self-esteem. Now he's found that he's not happy, he's insecure, and he doesn't have much self-respect. When his happiness no longer depends on how much money he has, how large his company is, and what he owns, he'll have taken a major step forward. When he no longer needs corporate toadies and dependent lovers to feel good about himself, he'll be more free.

One of the most powerful myths about money is that it equals power. This idea is particularly seductive because there is considerable truth to it: people with money do have a certain kind of power. That power can be used for good or bad, but regardless of the ultimate end, it's people's dependence on money for power that causes a psychological and spiritual problem.

If we believe that only our money gives us power or that we can't have power until we have money, we're cutting ourselves off from important parts of ourselves. We're limiting our experience of life in some very important ways. True power comes from who we are, not what we have. There are rich jerks and wonderful poor people. There are also poor jerks and wonderful rich people.

The other end of the spectrum—where people believe money is or should be completely unimportant—also has its traps. Many people avoid dealing with money out of fear of it, because they have contempt for it, because they feel it corrupts, because they fear success, or because money makes them feel things that conflict with how they see themselves.

Keith is an artist and speaks contemptuously of "money-grubbers." He's particularly sarcastic about the "salesperson mentality" he sees everywhere. He lives for the creation of his art and believes that money should be completely unimportant to him.

Keith has very little money and is constantly on the edge of financial ruin. Several of his relationships have ended over the issue of money as his partners realized that they could wind up supporting him.

We have an obligation to take care of ourselves and to help others who are in need. When people refuse to fulfill this obligation, it's often because of a hidden need to be dependent or to avoid having power. Not supporting yourself can also be related to a low sense of self-esteem.

Another common money myth is that having—or not having—money equals self-esteem. Many people have a negative self-image. They feel they're bad, or guilty of something, or undeserving, or worthless. If at the same time they believe that money·and success mean self-esteem, then having them would put them in conflict with their self-image. They'll avoid this conflict by avoiding success and money.

People with low self-esteem who believe that money and success are the source of self-esteem aren't likely to choose challenging careers, and they often avoid using their capabilities to the fullest extent. When they do have a chance to succeed, they often sabotage themselves in some way. They may choose to socialize with people their peers would find undesirable or even repellent. They're hiding from life, denying their potential. These success avoiders may strike a pose of having no attachment to money, but it's a false one. Their attachment is a negative one: avoidance.

EXERCISES

Write your answers to the following questions:

1. Is money relatively important or unimportant to you? How and when did you come to believe the way you do? How much of your belief comes from the impact of external conditions and how much from internal attitudes and beliefs?

2. Make a list of whatever you like to do the most. Try to list at least five activities.

- Which require money, and which don't? What people, places, and things are required for each one?

- Which ones have you done in the last three months? The last month? The last week? Which ones would you like to do more of? What people, places, and things, including money, would you need?

- Now look at the activities that require money. Are there ways to do these things that don't cost as much or that don't take money at all?

- Look at your spending for the last few months. Have you allocated too much money to these activities? Not enough money? Why?

3. Does money make you feel powerful or powerless? How does it accomplish this and why do you believe money equals power?

- Do you "moneypulate" others or do you let them do it to you? How do you use your power or let others use theirs on you?

- If power is the ability to accomplish your most cherished, deeply held personal goals, what do you need to accomplish them? If you need money to reach your goals, do you need more or do you have enough already?

4. What are the different kinds of power in the world? List people you know or know of who have each kind. What does it take to have each kind of power? Which attracts you, and why?

HOW COMFORTABLE WITH MONEY ARE YOU?

Very Uncomfortable   Very Comfortable
5—4—3—2—1—0—1—2—3—4—5

The second scale ranges from "Money makes me very uncomfortable" to "I am very comfortable with money." This scale is related to the myth that money equals happiness and security.

Some people are comfortable dealing with money and may even be fascinated by how it works. For others, money is a dark force, a source of profound discomfort. They become anxious merely thinking about making financial decisions.

Sally is a file clerk for a company that makes air-conditioning equipment. She's a single mother with two children and earns just enough for her family's basic expenses. Dealing with money has always made her uncomfortable, but she hasn't had to do more than watch her spending closely.

Sally's ex-husband finally started paying her alimony and child support. With a little extra money, she was facing some basic financial decisions, such as spending on things she'd like to have for the house versus building up an emergency fund. These decisions made her so uncomfortable that she couldn't even cash the checks.

She put the checks in a desk drawer and left them there for several months. If she didn't have to see them, she wouldn't have to think about them. Her ex-husband finally called to find out whether she'd gotten them—he'd noticed that they hadn't cleared his account. Now he's thinking about not sending more money.

———

1. Wherever you place yourself on the scale, what is it about money that makes you comfortable or uncomfortable? To what extent is your comfort or discomfort caused by externals, and to what extent by your attitudes and beliefs?

2. Are your feelings of comfort or discomfort with money related to any other parts of your psychology? Do your feelings confirm your self-image, or are they in conflict with it? How do these feelings relate to your social persona, the image you project to others?

3. If you're uncomfortable with money, what would it take for you to feel comfortable?

———

HOW DEPENDENT DOES MONEY MAKE YOU FEEL?

Dependent   Independent
5—4—3—2—1—0—1—2—3—4—5

The third scale ranges from "Money makes me feel interconnected and dependent" to "Money makes me feel independent and autonomous." As you place yourself on this scale, you may come to see your relationships, past and present, in a new light. Other variations on this scale include "Money makes me feel powerful or powerless" and "Money makes me feel in control or controlled by others or by circumstances."

This scale is particularly important in isolating some of the differences between the ways men and women are likely to relate to money. Because men and women tend to relate to power, security, and relationships differently, their relationships with money differ in the same ways.

Many couples' interpersonal issues are fought out on the battlefield of family finance. The real issues, however, come from the different emotional contexts within which they make financial decisions. When partners have different beliefs about money, and when those beliefs and the resulting behavior patterns are unconscious, it's easy for one person's behavior to threaten, limit, or undermine the other's needs.

One person's need for security can be another's loss of independence. One partner's expression of independence can undermine another's security. A use of money that makes one person feel capable and mature can make another feel insecure and childish.

When a couple can understand the emotional origins of a financial dispute and work with each other on that level, the need for the conflict often disappears. They can find ways to compromise and allow the other partner room to experience himself or herself in ways that build up a positive self-image.

Ed came from a very poor background and was strongly motivated by issues of security and control. His sense of self-worth was powerfully enhanced by his high level of retirement savings. He sacrificed constantly to be prepared for the future. Karen, his fiancée, came from a similar background but reacted to it differently. Her self-image revolved around feeling independent and autonomous, and spending money helped her feel that way.

Ed nagged Karen constantly about her spending. Karen criticized Ed for what she saw as his cheapness and his inability to enjoy himself. Their fights almost destroyed their relationship.

A counselor helped them see that their differing money psychologies were the reason for their conflict. Ed gradually understood that Karen's spending was her way of feeling adult and independent and that she perceived his nagging as an attempt to control her and undermine her autonomy. Karen learned that Ed wasn't a miser but acted out of a need for security and safety.

Now they can kid each other about their feelings. Ed has loosened up a bit and has even spent a little on himself. Karen has broadened her definition of adult behavior and has invested in a pension scheme. Now they compromise a bit and support each other, they say.

This scale is also related to the belief that money equals freedom. How often have you heard someone say, "If I just had enough money, I could do what I really want"? How often have you thought this yourself?

Bebe had always wanted to travel. She fantasized for years about a trip around the world. She put it off, thinking she could never afford it on a secretary's salary. Then she got fired. Surprising her friends and herself, Bebe took most of her life's savings and made the trip. "I just thought that if I didn't do it now, I'd never do it at all," she said. "I'll find another job when I get back, and you know, I bet it will be a better one."

It took the shock of being fired to get Bebe to change her thinking. She probably would never have taken the risk of quitting her job to travel, but getting fired removed the risk. Her decision to do what she'd always wanted empowered her and changed her estimate of the risk of spending her money on travel rather than finding another job right away.

The dependent side of the scale is also related to

the myth that money equals self-esteem. Without self-esteem, people often allow themselves to become dependent on others. They passively let themselves be defined in terms that fit their negative self-image. They may let a spouse or parent whom they know to be incompetent manage their finances. "Oh, I could never understand money," says Grace, a forty-five-year-old biologist. "I let Jim do that." Her husband, Jim, is a gambler and speculator who has twice lost their life savings on investments that didn't work out.

Financial dependency based on low self-esteem is strongly related to shame. When people with low self-esteem allow themselves to become dependent or act in ways that conform to their low self-images, the behavior is often accompanied by feelings of shame.

They see themselves acting in ways that have negative results. They conclude that there must be something wrong with them, that they must be to blame, and they feel ashamed of themselves. Shame is a self-perpetuating pattern. They believe a certain way, act on that belief, and feel ashamed. Their shame helps confirm their initial negative belief, and the cycle starts again.

EXERCISES

1. What would you do if you received a lot of money? Try to list at least five things. Where would you go, what activities would you do, what would you buy, and so forth? Take this exercise seriously. If you could do what you really wanted to, what would you do?

How much would it cost to do the things you've listed above? Find out if you don't know. Can you afford to do any of them now? If so, why haven't you done them already? If not, how long would it take to get enough money to do them? Do any of them not require money at all? Are there creative ways to do them that don't require as much money as you think?

2. What do you do or avoid doing with money to experience freedom, autonomy, dependence, or adulthood? (Your partner might be a great source of information for this one.)

- What other parts of your life do these patterns exist in? How do the patterns work in those areas? Do the other areas give you more information about how the patterns work with money?

- What is real freedom, real independence, real autonomy, real adulthood? What do these terms mean to you? What could you do in the next week, month, or three months to enhance your personal freedom, independence, autonomy, and adulthood?

- What has been keeping you from doing the things you've just listed? Consider your answer carefully. To what extent does it have anything to do with money?

HOW SECURE DOES MONEY MAKE YOU FEEL?

Insecure   Secure
5—4—3—2—1—0—1—2—3—4—5

This scale ranges from "Money makes me feel threatened and insecure" to "Money makes me feel safe and secure." Other versions of this scale include "Money makes me feel worthy or unworthy," and "Money makes me feel adequate or inadequate." This is one of the most powerful emotional scales, particularly in our planning for retirement and old age.

Fred became a successful psychologist. His income was more than £100,000 a year. The more money he made, though, the less secure he felt. He didn't think he really deserved his success, and he began sabotaging himself. His counseling wasn't as good as it once was. He started yelling at his staff, most of whom quit. His income has dropped significantly. Now less successful, Fred feels less insecure, so he's his old self again. His income is starting to grow. The cycle of success and self-defeat will repeat itself over and over.

Fred's experience is very common. Many people act in ways that get them just the opposite of what they think they want. Some people want relationships but drive others away as soon as they get close.

Some people want personal, athletic, professional, or business success but can't stand actually having it. They're more comfortable struggling for it or complaining about not having it. As they get close to success, their behavior changes in ways that guarantee failure.

The key to breaking out of this pattern is to see it as being driven by our internal needs rather than by external events. The road to change lies within, not in trying harder or waiting for the right chance or appropriate external conditions.

PARTIAL TRUTHS

Like the belief that money equals power, the identification of money with security has some truth to it. Money can provide the basic elements of physical security, food, shelter, and clothing as well as recreation and an aesthetically pleasing environment.

It's easy to go beyond our basic needs, however, and come to depend on having a certain amount of money for our personal security. If our entire feeling of safety comes from the amount of money we have, we're in a state of confusion. Money can't keep us from getting ill, or from aging and dying. It can't buy true friends and loving relationships. It can't keep us from being bored or unsatisfied. There's only one aspect of life that is permanent and unchanging: the Absolute.

REAL SECURITY

Inner security can't come from outside. It comes from having an integrated and strong sense of self and from one's connection with the Absolute.

Real security also comes from the individual's sense of self-worth. If we believe that self-worth is determined by how much money we have, we've made ourselves into slaves to money as well as to whatever might take it away from us.

Basing our security on money goes hand in hand with an insecure and fearful outlook on life. External conditions can change so rapidly. Money and other externals we depend on can disappear overnight. This realization makes people tense, defensive, and fearful.

But if our sense of self-worth *isn't* based on how much money we have, we're less vulnerable to what happens in the world. We can be more open and live without fear, because the things that happen, even if negative, don't threaten us on a deep inner level.

The ultimate source of security is our connection with the Divine. Living in that experience allows us to move beyond whatever happens to us. As with Christ, the Christian martyrs, the Sufi al-Hallaj, and some of the Jews who died in Nazi concentration camps, even the most terrible personal events can serve as a confirmation of faith and our connection with the Divine.

Answer the following questions in as much detail as possible. It's important to avoid judging yourself and to be as neutral an observer as possible.

1. How secure or insecure do you feel? What are the sources of your security or insecurity? To what extent are they connected with the amount of money you have or with how you feel about money?

2. Think of several people you know or know about who seem personally secure. What are the sources of their security? To what extent does their security depend on their financial condition?

3. If you believe money equals security and you have enough money to feel that secure, imagine yourself without money. What would it be like? How would you feel? Do these patterns of feeling exist in any other parts of your life?

4. If you believe money equals security but don't have enough to feel secure, decide how much money it would take for you to feel that way. Imagine having that amount of money. What would it be like? Would you feel differently about yourself? Imagine losing the money after having it. What would that be like?

How Does Money Affect Your Feeling of Existing?

Don't Exist   Exist
5—4—3—2—1—0—1—2—3—4—5

This scale ranges from "Money makes me feel I don't exist" to "Money makes me feel that I exist." This is one of the deepest and most basic aspects of our relationship with money and with ourselves. Many people feel, on a deep inner level, that they don't really exist.

They feel unrecognized by others and emotionally unconnected to their environment. They may also feel cut off from themselves. Taken together, these feelings, and lack of feeling, make them feel as if they're not there. This feeling is related to our sense of self-worth and how much we can allow ourselves to experience pleasure, happiness, and joy.

It's easy to use money to buy other people's attention. We can buy time with advisers and counselors. Many clients are simply paying for someone to really listen to them, since they feel unheard by others around them. Shopping and spending, however, play the same role for many others.

The shopper has a relationship, regardless of how shallow and temporary, with the salesperson. Even the act of paying for something involves being recognized by another human being. Just for a moment, someone else acknowledges us. Just for a moment, we exist for them, so we exist for ourselves.

Randi loves to shop. "I love being waited on," she says. "The salespeople know me and what I like, and they know I like to spend money, so they're glad to see me. They make me feel like I'm really someone." After a difficult day at work, when she's been in emotionally challenging situations, Randi is relieved to have someone come up to her and say, "How may I help you?" Randi's only problem is that she's hit her credit limit on all six credit cards, and the payments are becoming burdensome.

Randi has found a Twelve Step group for compulsive spenders and has been going to meetings for several months. "I thought no one else had the feelings I have," she says.

"Now I share my feelings in a safe environment, and I don't have to go shopping to feel better."

People can also spend money in their search for personal and social identity: "I'm a baseball card collector," "I'm a runner," "I'm a model train hobbyist," "I'm a skier," and so on. Each activity or involvement has a large and growing variety of goods and services you can buy to express and reinforce your identity. There's equipment, clothing, educational seminars, magazines, clubs to join, meetings to attend, emblems, and so forth. All require money.

The activity itself is not the problem, of course. The problem is our dependence on the activity for our personal identity.

People without much money often have no jobs or earn very little for their work. In a society where our income is often interpreted as the employer's (and society's) estimation of our worth, little or no income can mean that others don't value us.

If others don't value us, we may feel worthless. If we don't think we're worth anything in our society, we may feel that we don't exist. There's a lot of shame associated with these feelings, and low self-worth, shame, and fear often lead to violent behavior. Violence can be a way of forcing others to acknowledge our existence and a way of gaining power.

EXERCISES

1. Look back at the notes you've been making about how you feel when you buy things or spend money. What purchases or activities do you depend on for a sense of identity? How do these things contribute to your sense of yourself? What parts of yourself do you feel are affirmed? It's extremely important that you simply observe yourself without

judgment or self-blame. Your behavior isn't wro
simply trying to understand it.

2. Imagine being out of work, without prospects for new
employment. Visualize yourself in social situations, with others asking what you do for a living. What would it be like? How would you feel? Are your feelings based on others' reactions, your own ideas about how things should be, your reactions to what you see on television, or something else? What beliefs about money do these effects depend on?

CONCLUSION

As you place yourself on these scales, you'll begin to see the meanings you've given to money. Perhaps money means power and control, or autonomy and independence. Perhaps it means powerlessness and inadequacy.

It would take an encyclopedic work to detail all the patterns of meaning money has for people. The purpose of this book isn't to study them all but to help you find out what your money patterns are, so you can change them if they don't work for you and enhance them if they do.

The next step is to break the hold your undesirable beliefs have over you and give you tools to deal with money in a more balanced and rational way.

CHAPTER FIVE

HEALING YOUR MONEY WOUNDS

Question: What is two plus two?
Answer: Are you buying or selling?
—Lebanese folk saying

As you've worked through the preceding chapters, you've taken important steps toward a full awareness of your relationship with money. You've had a chance to begin understanding the meanings you've given to money and the ways those meanings make you feel. You've also examined the childhood origins of your beliefs and attitudes. Understanding is just the first step, however.

As we begin to experience some space between our old responses and our current behavior, we have an opportunity to change the way we act with and around money. We can adjust our behavior so that it becomes more appropriate for us. Our behavior can become harmonious with our real personal values and can serve our growth as human beings.

A BAD CONNECTION

When we associate money with security, love, respect, self-worth, and other basic needs, we are likely to overreact to situations involving money. Our behavior tends to be inappropriate and ineffective: inappropriate, because money can never permanently satisfy these needs; and ineffective, because we're not getting what we want and because we're probably not making good financial decisions along the way! We can work hard, earn a lot, save a lot, spend a lot, invest a lot, and still not feel safe, secure, loved, respected, and worthy. The harder we try to fill the empty spaces inside us with money and what it can buy, and the more we use it to keep fear and self-doubt at bay, the more trouble we encounter.

Our personality types, our choice of career, our behavior at work, the recreational activities we prefer, our relationships with family and friends, and our spiritual lives—all are powerfully affected by the beliefs and attitudes toward money that we have identified in the preceding chapters.

The purpose of this chapter is to help you assess your behavior so you can decide whether it serves you or not. It will also give you exercises to change the way you feel, think about, and act with money.

———

SELF-ASSESSMENT

Write out your answers to the following questions. As you do so, consider what they reveal about your particular behavioral patterns with money. Then you can connect this understanding with your understanding of the meanings you've given to money and of the childhood origins of those beliefs. The light of this insight will give you the opportunity to change.

It's important for you to do these exercises without self-judgment. It's also important to consider your true feelings, not what you think your family and friends expect of you or what you think you should feel or believe.

1. If you suddenly inherited a lot of money or won the lottery, what would be your first impulse? Your second? Would

your life be any different than it is now? Would you be any different?

2. Do you worry about money? What are your specific worries? How serious are they?

3. Do you have specific financial goals? If you haven't written them down explicitly, do so now. How do you feel when you consider them? If you don't have financial goals, how would having them make you feel?

4. Do you have a monthly or yearly budget? If so, do you follow it? If not, how would having a budget make you feel?

5. Do you enjoy shopping and spending money on yourself? On others? Is spending difficult for you? Do you spend impulsively or compulsively? What causes it, and how do you feel during and afterward?

6. Do you hoard things? Do you have spares for everything? Do you save a lot but have difficulty investing in any but the most conservative investment vehicles?

7. Do you keep good financial records? How do you feel when you're working on them? Do you balance your checkbook? If you don't keep good records, how would keeping them make you feel?

8. Do you save money? Do you save for the future, or for specific luxury items? If you don't save, how would saving make you feel?

9. Do you know how much income it would take to satisfy you completely? If so, is this more or less than you're making now? How would it feel to be suddenly earning just that amount?

10. Do you have any investments? How do you feel about taking risks? Do you enjoy learning about investing? Do you enjoy making investment decisions, or do you prefer to turn them over to others?

11. Are you happy with your work? Are you paid what you're worth? Would you be happier earning more than you do now? Would you feel better earning less than you do now?

12. If you have a spouse or partner, is his or her attitude toward money the same as yours? How are you similar or different? Do you disagree or fight with your partner about money-related issues?

13. How do you feel about paying your income tax? About paying your bills? Do you ever cheat or delay as long as possible? If so, how do you feel about it?

14. Do you give your children an allowance? Do they have to work for it? Must they account for what they do with it? Do you take it away as punishment? What do you teach them about money? Is this the same or different from the way your parents treated you?

15. How has answering these questions made you feel? Are you happy you've done them correctly or afraid you haven't done a good enough job? Are you anxious because of the

issues they've raised, or are you laughing at the absurdity of it all?

MONEY WOUNDS

When we're physically wounded, our body's integrity has been violated. Blood, which should have been circulating to maintain our body's natural state, leaks out. Our body is weakened, and if the bleeding isn't stopped, we may eventually die.

Emotional wounds function the same way. Emotional energy, which would ordinarily be available for the normal and healthy functioning of our personality, can be drained away by a conflict or concern. We're weakened and have less energy for normal moment-to-moment thoughts, feelings, and reactions. Some people become almost entirely unresponsive, without the energy to react to what happens to them.

Money can wound us deeply, because the beliefs and behaviors we've adopted often don't get us what we want. They can lead us to self-defeating behavior, which has exactly the opposite effect of what we intend. The way out is to adopt behavior that is in harmony with our deeply held personal values. Then we will be moving toward what we want in life, and our behavior will be in harmony with our goals.

RIDING THE GREED/FEAR CYCLE

The bumper sticker on Hal's car reads, "The one who dies with the most toys wins." Hal believes this deeply, and he works very hard selling copiers and fax machines because he knows he can make a lot of money quickly. He has the focus and dedication of a professional athlete. His home resembles a catalog of all the latest gadgets and equipment, and he loves having whatever's new on the market.

Dick's intelligence and abilities are way above average.

Despite this, he's never looked for challenging work. "I just don't want to be bothered with all that," he says. "It's too much work to be out there grubbing after success."

Both Hal's and Dick's lives are dominated by money. The only difference is that the form of the relationship is different. Hal is dominated by an attraction to money, and Dick by a fear of it. In both cases, the meanings of money have become a way of covering up an inner pain.

Hal has extremely low self-esteem. He can't believe anyone would like him for himself. He surrounds himself with the latest and most expensive toys so he can gain people's interest and admiration and distract them from noticing what he's really like.

Dick doesn't think he's worthy of success. He doesn't believe in himself. He's so convinced of this that he won't even try to get ahead, although he covers it up with a contempt for others' efforts. If he were to succeed, he'd have to change his self-image, and he has so identified with it that change is not very likely without some powerful efforts for growth on his part.

Many of us are stuck at our current level of emotional and spiritual growth. We'll grow no further unless we confront the limitations we've placed on ourselves. Regardless of the work we try to do on ourselves, or how much we achieve, if we don't confront these limiting beliefs and behaviors we won't experience deep personal growth.

Whether we're dominated by greed or fear, investing appropriately can be a problem. Greedy people can take too much risk. They're unwilling to take the long-term approach that's far more likely to work. They may invest all their money in one high-risk stock. They may chase scheme after scheme, with little analysis of their real chance of success. They want to get rich but aren't willing to do it slowly.

Fearful people are often so scared of short-run investment risk that they take high levels of long-run risk. Since any fluctuation in the value of their investments scares them deeply, they keep most or all of their money in bank savings and investment accounts where there is very little risk of losing their money, but also a very low rate of return. They actually lose by investing this way; the leading long-run risks are taxes and inflation, not fluctuations in value. They will have far less purchasing power than they should have, in some cases less than when they invested.

ARE WE MONEYPULATED?

The advertising industry knows we make financial decisions on the basis of our deep emotional needs. Advertisers have learned to manipulate the buying public by appealing to these needs in order to sell anything and everything. The negative aspect of this is, of course, that to the extent that we buy goods and services to satisfy our emotional needs, our money is unavailable for our longer-term goals, such as education for ourselves and our children, retirement, and so on

The underlying message in almost all advertising is that "You're not enough." We aren't good enough men, women, spouses, lovers, mothers, or fathers. We could be having more fun. We could be getting more out of life. And we can be more, have more, get more, if we just buy this product.

This moneypulation helps convince us that the way to satisfy our deep inner needs is to spend money. It can convince us that what we buy and what we do are the sources of our identity. It turns our eyes outward.

We learn to use our possessions and activities instead of our sense of self to satisfy our needs for survival, power, love, fulfillment, security, and self-esteem. We give away our power over our inner lives, in return for an endless search in the outer world. We allow ourselves to be dominated by money, without realizing that we can break the pattern whenever we want to.

WE HAVE MET THE ENEMY . . .

Think of people you know whose behavior—in any part of their lives—is self-defeating. The result of how they act is that they get the opposite of what they want. An example might be the person who desperately wants an intimate relationship but whose behavior turns others off. This is what too often happens with regard to money. We behave in ways that end up making us feel threatened and insecure.

. . . AND THEY IS US

Now you can look at your own behavior through the understanding of your relationship with money that you've gained so far. You can look at how you earn, spend, save, invest, and use money in relationships, and you can start to change whatever behavior you find limiting or self-defeating. Along the way, you'll also find it easier to make good financial decisions.

THE MONEY TREADMILL

Most of us want to feel safe, secure, loving, loved, and worthy. However, many people depend on money to fulfill these needs. Money can't permanently satisfy these needs, so these people put themselves on a treadmill. They work harder and harder in an exercise that, while it may increase their capacity to work hard, won't get them where they want to go.

WORK, WORK, SPEND, SPEND

The "W2S2" pattern demands more and more energy. We get more and more stuff, do more and more things, and may even acquire more and more wealth. The only things we don't get are real security, safety, a sense of being loved, and self-esteem—in other words, our original motivations! This is the quest for fool's gold.

We have only to go to a local bookstore to see all the books that help us drive ourselves to higher and higher levels of effort in the search for fool's gold. Books on success, achievement, time management—if we could just work harder, learn the right techniques, then our efforts would get us what we really want! Harder, faster, harder, faster! Get on the treadmill!

If what we're doing to earn money doesn't satisfy our inner needs, doing it more efficiently won't either. If the things we've bought haven't made us feel better, buying more of them won't help. And if saving and investing haven't made us feel safe, perhaps we should look elsewhere for our security.

MONEY BEHAVIOR

This chapter groups behavior with money around three main issues: success and failure, spending and saving, and relationships with others. The discussions of these aspects of money behavior will show how problems in these areas lead to poor personal financial decisions. Each section contains exercises you can use to change undesirable behavior and make better financial decisions.

As you read about and assess the behaviors described below, remember that the behavior itself isn't the problem. The problem is the disconnection between people's values (what they want) and the results of the behavior (what they get).

SUCCESS AND FAILURE

Because we tend to define success and failure in financial terms, our attitudes toward money are powerfully interrelated with our behavior as we work toward or avoid success. The same attitudes are also activated when we experience failure.

There's nothing wrong with financial success, of course. It's the individual's attitude toward it that matters. If we rely on success for our self-image, or if we depend on the money and what it buys for our sense of self-worth, then we have a problem. Our quest has been for fool's gold.

Frances *is* what she does. She's a management consultant and helps organizations restructure themselves in healthier ways. She believes passionately in her work and feels good about herself when she can do more of it. When business slacks off, she tends to indulge herself by overeating and by compulsive shopping. Her goal is to build a large firm and become a national figure in her field. She doesn't have much time for friends or relationships. She says she'll "catch up later, when everything's in place."

Harvey works hard to avoid success. He's a solicitor and has worked at three major firms. He's been considered for partnership at each one, but each time his behavior has changed, much to the confusion of his family, friends, and co-workers. He's become crude and offensive, very much unlike his usual manner. When the opportunity passes, Harvey reverts to his normal behavior. He's unaware that he changes at all and has grown more bitter as each opportunity disappears.

We tend to structure our lives in accordance with our inner view of ourselves. Frances needs more and more success to support her positive self-image. When she doesn't get the chance to support it that way, she finds other ways, such as eating and spending. Harvey avoids success because it would conflict with his negative self-image. Neither he nor Frances is free. Both are captives of their unmet inner needs.

There's nothing wrong with becoming a national figure in one's field. There's nothing wrong with becoming a partner in one's law firm—or with not wanting to be one. But chasing after things to satisfy needs that can't be met even by success—that's a fool's game.

Chasing success becomes particularly self-defeating when

we don't like what we're doing but keep doing it anyway because it offers the possibility of success. This self-brutalization can result in all sorts of problems. Addictive or compulsive use of alcohol, other drugs, sex, exercise, spending, and other activities can serve as escapist outlets for the unsatisfied emotional energy and anger that can build up in a situation like this.

EXERCISES

1. Write down the major successes and failures in your life. What were your feelings as you experienced each? How did you feel affirmed or threatened in each case? Exactly what did you do or not do that brought you each result? How do you feel now, looking back on each experience? Does each one seem as important to you today as it did at the time? Do you feel the same or differently about each one now?

2. Look carefully at all the things you have bought in your life. Which ones symbolize success or failure to you? What is it about them—or you—that makes this so? What are the things you yearn for that would make you feel successful? What is it about them that would make you feel that way? Can you think of any other way you could get that feeling that would not require you to spend much money?

3. How much would be "enough" for you? What would it take for you to feel satisfied with your level of material existence? Write down the things you want but don't have. Be careful not to go beyond a sense of enough. An example might be wanting a large screen television but not needing a TV in your bedroom and basement as well.

4. How successful do you feel—in your work, in your personal relationships, and in your personal growth? Place yourself on the following continuum, which ranges from total failure to success beyond your dreams.

Failure   Success
5—4—3—2—1—0—1—2—3—4—5

What is it about each part of your life that makes you feel successful or unsuccessful? What would have to change for you to move in a positive direction on the scale? Are these changes within your control or beyond it?

What are your goals in each part of your life: work, financial, family and personal relationships, community, physical, spiritual? What would you *really* like to achieve? Write your goals down as explicitly as possible. Describe what you want to achieve and when you want to achieve it. How do your goals relate to your attitudes toward success?

SPENDING AND SAVING

Spending money is perhaps the archetypal financial activity in our lives. Shopping is almost our national sport, and "When the going gets tough, the tough go shopping," our motto. Ninety-three percent of teenage girls report that shopping is their favorite activity.* Traffic reports in many areas routinely include information about conditions near malls—huge, indoor shopping complexes—as well as roads to the beach, the lake, or other major attractions. The largest tourist attraction in the state of Virginia is an outlet mall.

In August 1992, the Mall of America opened in Minnesota. It's a mile around and four stories tall, with its own

*Alan Thein Durning, "What Malls and Materialism Are Doing to the Planet," *Washington Post* (August 23, 1992):C3.

seven-acre indoor amusement park. People come from all over the world just to see this mega-monument to consumerism. It symbolizes a life-style of consumption for its own sake.

Malls have become the new neighborhoods. In most urban areas, people used to go to certain neighborhoods to walk around, eat in one of the many restaurants, look at the shops, see a movie, and just be around and watch other people. In today's suburbia, few such districts exist, and the few that do aren't as safe as they once were. Like the self-enclosed cities of science fiction novels, malls have become domed neighborhoods, protected from the weather and the social elements outside.

People of all ages now go to malls for entertainment. They look at the shops, eat in the restaurants, meet each other, and go to movies. Older people walk for exercise. There are even shoes designed for this, called "mall walkers." People take their children to the mall and leave them for an afternoon, knowing they'll be safe.

These activities integrate shopping and buying even more closely with other social activities. Spending money becomes ever more interrelated with the satisfaction of various human needs. Life becomes something we consume rather than experience.

And, of course, we can't afford all of the buying—as individuals, as a nation, or as a planet. As individuals we need to save and invest more for retirement. As a nation we must invest more in creating new productive capacity, and we must spend less on current consumption. On a planetary basis, we have an obligation to come to a sense of "enoughness" that gives us personal satisfaction but consumes less of the world's resources than we presently do.

By making the Mall of America a symbol of the world's

desired life-style, we tragically mislead ourselves and those who hope to someday have what we do. There simply aren't enough resources for the entire world to live a high-consumption life-style. At some point the world must reach a compromise. The question will be, How much is enough?

THE PSYCHOLOGY OF SPENDING

There are people who have money and people who are rich.
—Coco Chanel

The way we feel about spending is related to our attitude toward security, our attempts to validate our self-image and social persona, and our willingness to enjoy ourselves. And our spending behavior automatically determines our saving behavior, since these compete for our income.

Saving and investing take money from current consumption and divert it to future consumption. Spending uses money today and thus costs future consumption. Each use of money has its cost in terms of the other.

When the meanings we give to money demand inappropriately high levels of current spending, we're denying ourselves the future security we could have had. When our money psychology demands excessive preparation for the future, we're fulfilling our need for security at the cost of enjoyment today. It's not the spending or the saving itself that's the problem. It's how we come to the particular balance we've struck.

We can choose to spend a moderate amount in affirmation of our self-image and to project our desired social persona. At the same time, we can save an amount that will generate the level of income we want to retire on, to put our children through college, or to get us to our other long-term goals. This balance will be different for everyone. The important thing is that our spending and saving balance should be a conscious one.

———

1. Add up, as best you can, the total sum you've earned so far in your life. How much of that income did you save? How much do you still have? Project your income for the rest of your life. How much will you earn, and how much would you like to save?

2. Create a budget for a model spending month. Build in savings for your non-monthly expenditures, such as car insurance. Also build in savings for your long-term goals, even if you're already contributing to your pension at work. Use this month as a yardstick for the rest of the year. When you find yourself deviating from it, make sure there's a good reason for the change.

If you can't bring yourself to use a formal budget and you still want to save, here's the "short form." Each time you get paid, and before you pay any bills, simply write a check for 5 percent of your income to your savings program. Then live however you like on the rest. If 5 percent doesn't seem to hurt, try 6 percent. If that doesn't seem to make a difference, increase it to 7 percent. Keep increasing the saving until you start running out of money before getting paid again.

3. If you have trouble spending on yourself, you probably also have trouble enjoying yourself. Once a week, go to a mall or other shopping area. Your goal is to spend a small sum on yourself, say ten pounds. You must make five separate purchases, however. They can't be food or

anything you need for daily use, like underwear or socks. You shouldn't leave until you reach your goal.

4. Consider the fulfillment you get from each expenditure you make. Which expenditures are the most useful? The most enjoyable? Which give you less pleasure? Is there some level of spending beyond which you get less and less enjoyment?

5. Use checks for as many purchases as possible. Using a credit card, even if you pay it off at the end of the month, is a less conscious act than writing a check. Writing a check takes more time than using cash or a credit card. It requires more physical effort. You have to write down the amount you're spending and where. You may write the amount as many as three times, twice on the check and once in the register. Because all this slows you down, using checks can help you be more conscious as you spend.

6. You and your spouse or partner should compare the meanings that spending and saving have for each of you. Understand the needs these activities satisfy. Try not to judge each other. If your needs differ, perhaps there are ways you can compromise so both partners' needs can be met.

MONEYPULATOR OR MONEYPULATED?

Money can affect relationships in many ways. Our feelings about money, love, and power may be intimately intertwined. We may seek power or avoid it. We may enjoy dominating others or being dominated by them. Any of these relationships can be an expression of our self-image and thus satisfy our needs.

Many people express love by spending money on the object of their affections. This attitude makes our ability to love hostage to the amount of money we have. People may also measure the extent of their partner's (or prospective partner's) love by how much money is being spent on them. This attitude narrows the range of prospective partners, to say the least.

Bob always picks up the check. He often buys his family and friends expensive gifts he knows they can't afford on their own. He gives his wife, whom he has pressed not to work, a weekly allowance.

Victor knows his wife is a poor money manager. Nonetheless, she manages their finances. They lurch from catastrophe to catastrophe, but Victor won't take over. "I could never do that," he says. "I don't want to be running things—this is a partnership."

THE NEW GOLDEN RULE:
THE ONE WITH THE GOLD MAKES THE RULES

The ways we use power and feel powerful reflect certain emotional patterns. Not everyone who has power feels powerful. Many people overuse their power to compensate for feelings of powerlessness and inferiority. Some people, of course, use power to confirm their self-image of superiority and greater self-worth more than others.

Money is a potent tool in our relationship with the world. It can confer power. We can use money to command others' time and energy. Our money can place us in certain social hierarchies, to our pleasure or dismay.

If we wish, we can allow others to dominate us with money. Since there are many people who need to do this, we can find willing partners if we desire this role in a relationship.

THE NEW FREEDOM?

There are more and more books being published on how to free ourselves from our current life pattern and become more independent. If we do what we like, we're told, the money will follow. Not only is this untrue, it's profoundly misleading. We can be as wonderfully creative as possible in some areas, and we'll still never make much money.

Creativity and freedom are more than strategies for making more money. The point this approach misses is that the growth that results from freeing ourselves from the inner and outer restrictions we've accepted in the past is its own reward. When we choose work that flows from the heart, our enhanced experience of life is our reward. That's what we sacrifice for. If we do make more money, fine. But if we break the patterns of the past just for more money, we're merely changing the furniture in our prison cell.

———

EXERCISES

1. Consider someone who has a great deal of personal power but little or no money. Now consider someone who has money but little personal power. What are the differences between them?

2. What would you like to have the power to accomplish in your life? What would you have to do to reach these goals? How many of the steps you would have to take would require money?

3. If you use money to dominate others or as proof of your love, list several activities you enjoy doing that don't require money. Can you do these with other people? When was the last time you did? Put yourself on a schedule and

do them as much as possible, noting your feelings as you do them. Do others react to you differently than before?

4. If you allow others to dominate you with money, list several activities you enjoy doing that don't require money. Try to participate in these with individuals who've dominated you with money in the past. Note your feelings and their reactions.

5. Return to the goals you listed earlier in this chapter. List the intermediate steps you will have to take to reach each one. Now look at each intermediate step. What needs to be done first to complete that step? What should be done next? List the tasks to be completed for each step.

6. Learn the basics of personal financial management. Read books, take a course, do whatever it takes—it isn't rocket science. See pages 167-168 for a list of books that can help you along. Check with your library, local community college, adult education programs, and your local paper for courses in your area.

7. Start an investment program. Contribute to your pension if you aren't already. Increase your contribution if you can. If you're already maximizing your pension contribution, open an account with a mutual fund that invests primarily in stocks.

Study the mutual fund's annual report. Look at the list of stocks in the fund's portfolio. How many production, distribution, and administrative facilities do you think each company on the list has? How many states and different countries are they located in? How many people work for each company? How many people buy and use each company's products?

How many other products are produced using those the companies make? How does it feel to be part of this vast network of interrelated economic functions?

If you've invested in certificates of deposit, consider the loans the banks have made with your money. If you've invested in government securities, consider what the government's done with your money. Do the same for any corporate or municipal bonds you own. Consider your feelings about participating in these economic patterns and institutions.

————

Conclusion

By freeing ourselves of the behavior patterns that supported our money wounds, we're giving ourselves the opportunity to heal. By starting on the road toward our real goals in life, we're opening the door to happiness.

The next step is to identify our most deeply held personal values. When we have a clear understanding of what we care about most, we'll be able to decide what's right and wrong for us. We'll understand quickly and easily whether or not a job, relationship, purchase, or course of action is in our best interest. And we'll see if our goals, whether financial or in other parts of our lives, are what we really want.

Our values will also show us how to get the most satisfaction out of life. They'll describe the path we should take in whatever area of life we focus on. Examining our values can be the door to personal and spiritual growth.

CHAPTER SIX

LIVING YOUR PERSONAL VALUES

Let the beauty you love be what you do.
—Rumi

The first step toward living spiritually is to live in harmony with our most deeply held personal values. They can be the bridge between our personal lives and our spiritual lives. Many people spend their lives just reacting to what happens to them. They're trapped in their unconscious, habitual patterns of thought and behavior.

Living spiritually means breaking free of those deeply ingrained patterns so that a new force can manifest itself. The process of freeing ourselves isn't easy. One way to start is to reorient our lives by building on the things we believe in most strongly.

Robert was married, with two young children. He'd worked as an auto mechanic for seven years and made a good living. As he watched his children grow, he considered his future as well. The more he thought, the less he wanted to continue as he had. "There's nothing wrong with being a mechanic," he says. "I liked working with my hands and fixing people's cars so they run well again. But there's this part of me that wasn't satisfied, and I got more and more unhappy with my life. I wasn't happy at home or at work."

Robert thought very deeply and realized that one of his most important needs was to make a real difference in other people's lives. The more he thought about it, the more he felt called to help other people on a one-on-one basis. He decided to become a counselor. He has gone back to college part-time, and he'll get a master's degree in social work after he finishes his bachelor's degree.

Robert says the decision to change careers changed other parts of his life. "I'm a better husband and father now. My attitude is different," he explains. "I'm not just living for myself and my family. I feel more positive, more in control of my fate. My kids are too young to tell me how they feel, but I can see they know I've changed. I really feel renewed."

The ability to live what we believe is very important. It makes what we hold in our hearts the source of how we behave and what we do. It gives us a way of evaluating options and choosing between alternative courses of action. "Should I do this or that? What do I really want? What will serve me best in the long run?"—these are questions we can answer if we have a clear set of personal values.

By making our lives more conscious, acting on the basis of our values helps us create a foundation for spiritual growth. As we clarify our values and become aware of the extent to which our lives match them, we'll find our level of self-awareness growing enormously. That growth in awareness will serve us well as we work more specifically later on.

DON'T BE A SPIRITUAL WANNABE

Believing in spirituality doesn't make us spiritual. Thinking spiritual thoughts doesn't make us spiritual. Rituals, prayers, exercises, and meditation aren't enough. Just knowing about a spiritual tradition won't work either. Psychic powers are abilities, not spirituality.

Being spiritual means getting our egos out of the way so the Absolute can express itself through where "we" used to be. Spiritual work is whatever reduces our ego's demands on life, whatever frees us of our efforts to control people, places, and things so we can get what we want and avoid pain.

LIVING WITH AN ATTITUDE

Have you ever been told you have an attitude problem? To a pilot, the word *attitude* refers to the angle at which the plane meets the wind. Are the wings level? Is the plane climbing or descending? The plane's attitude determines its direction.

Our attitude is the way we meet the daily challenges our life brings us. Our beliefs, expectations, and values determine the way we hold ourselves in relation to the constant flow of experiences we call living. Our attitude determines how we'll meet that flow, the direction we'll go in, how we'll feel along the way, and where we'll wind up.

A negative attitude will tend to produce a negative experience of life. Those with negative attitudes rarely perform at the level they're truly capable of. Why should they? They expect that things won't work out.

Beth is an "energy vampire." All she ever talks about is her problems and the bad things that happen to her. All she wants to hear about is others' problems and the bad things that happen to them. She drains energy from those around her rather than supporting them and helping them meet the challenges they face. They feel depressed after speaking with her.

Beth expects everything to go wrong, and it usually does. She's lost several jobs in the last two years, and she can't seem to keep friends for long. She doesn't understand why this happens. She thinks it's because "things always go wrong for me."

Beth doesn't understand that her constant focus on the negative is an expression of her sense of powerlessness and of being a victim. Her expectation that the same conditions will apply to everyone makes it harder for people around her to deal with their lives. If they discuss their feelings with Beth, she tells them their efforts won't work, affirms how difficult doing anything is, and, without meaning to, demeans their efforts to learn or maintain a positive attitude toward themselves.

YOU'LL SEE IT WHEN YOU BELIEVE IT

Attitudes are self-reinforcing. A negative attitude tends to produce negative results. If we expect things to go wrong, they probably will. When things do go wrong, our expectations will have been confirmed. Our experience will have proven us right. Our attitude will be self-defeating, but we'll have had the pleasure of having been right.

Our values and attitudes are a matter of choice. Positive values and a positive attitude will tend to produce positive results. Those with positive attitudes will perform closer to the highest level they're capable of. Their positive expectations allow them to mobilize more of their energies, work with greater intensity, and be more creative. They put more into their efforts and get more out of them.

When we're supportive of others' efforts to reach their goals, we generally get support from others to reach ours. We build a network of support and positive energy that confirms our positive values and attitude. Our experience confirms our values and attitude. We too will have been proven right.

WHAT IS A VALUE?

Values are strongly held principles of belief and behavior. We might value strength, or honesty, or spirituality. Personal values function as unifying or governing principles, because we can apply them to all parts of our lives. These principles unify the different aspects of our lives by helping us to experience them and respond to them in a consistent fashion.

If we value honesty highly, we'll seek to be honest in every way we can. We'll judge ourselves by the extent to which we're able to be honest, and we'll appear honest to others. Those who value honesty will be attracted to us.

Values aren't goals. A goal is a result, something to be attained. A value is a principle, a quality. Our goal might be to lose ten pounds, while the value involved might be self-discipline or self-esteem. Reaching the goal would be the result of expressing the value.

Every moment gives us another opportunity to experience and express our values. Regardless of our previous success or failure, each moment is a new chance. Success is never permanent, but neither is failure. Each moment of life is a challenge and an opportunity. As we respond, we increase our ability to continue responding. We become more "response-able." If we don't respond, our ability to do so can begin to weaken and become useless, like an unused muscle.

By discovering our values and living them, we can gain a sense of control and commitment, and realize the joy of being challenged. Our values will tell us what's important and what isn't. It's like being on a journey and having a map and compass for guidance.

DEFAULT VALUES
We are never without values. When we don't choose the highest values we can, we accept others by default. We might believe, consciously or unconsciously, that whatever makes us feel good is good, or that whatever makes us feel powerful is good. When we accept this, we've defaulted to lower and less conscious values. On the other hand, the more conscious our choice, the more powerful the value becomes for us.

Values are windows through which we view our lives. When we meet people who don't share the same values, we find that they view life very differently than we do. It's not that they're consciously interpreting things differently. They simply don't see things the way we do.

THE MEANING OF MEANING
Values give meaning to experience. They help us under-

stand what we perceive. How do we interpret the behavior of others? How should we react to what others do and say? How do we know what to do? How do we know what's important in life? How do we make the many choices we're faced with all the time? Our personal values allow us to see meaning in what goes on around us.

Harvey and Sheila were first attracted to each other's values. "We were at a business meeting," Harvey says, "and I noticed how Sheila said what she really believed. She didn't let her boss intimidate her, and she didn't hide what she really thought. I really like that in a person."

"Harvey came up to me after a meeting," says Sheila. "He said he was attracted to me and told me why. He was very direct and honest. I like that in a man."

Our values give us the power to make our lives meaningful. We're always aware, on some level, of the extent of harmony or conflict between what we believe and what we do. When what we believe is in harmony with how we behave, our experience of life is full of meaning. As we act, we experience the things we believe in most, and our lives are therefore meaningful.

Our values are the foundation of our attitude. The unifying principles we accept determine our beliefs about life, our expectations, and the way we interpret what we experience.

There is no need to run outside for better seeing,
nor to peer from a window.
Rather abide at the center of your being,
for the more you leave it,
the less you learn.
—Lao Tzu

THE GREATER HARMONY OF VALUES

Values also offer us a way to connect with others. We can experience our family, friends, community, and society by sharing their values. Shared values lead to shared meaning and a common understanding of life. Even when personal experiences differ, common values lead to a sense of meaning that is the same.

We may or may not choose to accept the values of our family, friends, community, or nation. But by understanding others on the basis of their values, we'll become able to see their lives as they do. We'll know them as they know themselves and their lives. This understanding is the basis for compassion, forgiveness, and unconditional love.

DISCOVERING YOUR VALUES

To live more consciously, we must ultimately choose the values we want to live by. The following list includes values identified by Dr. Emmett Miller, a physician and specialist in self-hypnosis and motivation, as well as others. It's not all-inclusive, of course. Let these examples serve as a starting point for your responses to the exercises that follow.

Potential Personal Values

Achievement	Fun
Adventure	God
Beauty	Growth
Brotherhood	Happiness
Charity	Health
Community	Honesty
Creativity	Honor
Dignity	Humility
Family	Independence
Friendship	Individuality

Potential Personal Values

Integrity	Reason
Intimacy	Respect
Justice	Security
Kindness	Self-Discipline
Knowledge	Self-Esteem
Leadership	Service
Love	Spirituality
Patriotism	Strength
Peace	Supportiveness
Positivity	Surrender
Power	Trust
Pride	Truth
	Wisdom

EXERCISES:

DISCOVERING YOUR VALUES

1. Think back to the best things that ever happened to you. Try to list at least ten. Perhaps they were times that you were at your best, when you achieved a great deal or succeeded beyond your expectations. Perhaps they involved relationships with other people. What was it about each experience that made it so good for you? What do these experiences tell you about your values?

2. Ask yourself the following questions:

- What is most important to you in life? What does your conscience tell you your highest priorities should be?

- If you could live your life exactly as you know you should, how would that be? What values would you have, and how would you express them? To avoid responding too simply or too abstractly, do the following: When answering this question, sit comfortably, at a time and place that give you privacy. Use your senses to imagine yourself with the life you want. See yourself, hear what's going on, smell the smells, feel what's touching you, experience the emotions. Make it as rich an inner experience as you can.

- List all the values you care about. If you could live only four or five of them completely, which would they be? Which principles will give you the highest payoff, the most positive results over your lifetime? These are your most important governing values, your unifying principles. Write a short paragraph describing what each value means to you. Express each one in "I am" form. Example: "I am creative . . . , I am . . ."

- How would you, your family, your friends, your community, your nation, and the world suffer if you didn't live in harmony with your governing values? Write your answer in as much detail as possible.

3. Use your governing values to examine your behavior over the last year. To what extent have you lived in harmony with your values? How has your behavior not expressed or been in conflict with your values? Have you felt differently when your behavior expressed your values than when it didn't? How? Write your answers to these questions. Begin a "values journal," and use it to better understand your values and bring your behavior into greater harmony with them.

4. Make your behavior a better expression of your governing values. Learn to be who you really are. Spend five minutes each morning focusing on your values. Consider the whole group or focus on one value each day. Values are

like precious gems with many facets: you can see something new each time you look.

Remember, your governing values are who you really are. To get a lot from these exercises, you have to put a lot of emotional intensity into them. You have to *care.*

5. Go on a retreat once in a while. Get away from everything for a morning, an afternoon, or a day. Think about your behavior. Has it expressed your highest understanding of your values? Has it fallen short? How? Why? Write your answers in your journal. It's important to do this without judgment. If you beat yourself up, you make it harder on yourself. It's a paradox, in a way: you have to care very deeply but not punish yourself for failing. Treat yourself the way you'd treat someone you care about very much.

6. What are your goals for the next year? The next five years? What do you want to achieve in your lifetime? Make a list of what you want to do, experience, and achieve in each time frame.

7. What are the intermediate steps you'll have to take to reach each goal? How long will it take you to get each one done? Do the intermediate steps themselves have inter- mediate steps? Choose one of your goals for the next year. What could you do in the next three months to move toward it? The next month? The next week?

There are many good books on time management and how to achieve your goals. The Daytimer, Franklin Planner and Filofax datebook systems are among the best available. Choose whichever resources appeal most to you and start using them.

Conclusion

Remember, your governing values are not goals by themselves. Your values will be the qualities of your efforts to reach your goals. They'll help you make the decisions you'll face along the way. If a potential decision, action, or alternative is in harmony with your governing values, it's worth your consideration. If it's not, then pursuing it would violate the beliefs you hold most dear. The word for this is *hypocrisy.*

Your goals should be an expression of your governing values. They should be realistic and as clear and specific as possible, with an explicit time dimension. And you have to believe in them passionately. You have to be able to see, feel, hear, smell, and taste what it would be like to achieve them.

This is where those who achieve great things differ from those who never do. The achievers can imagine themselves reaching their goals. The failures or "never-triers" cannot.

CHAPTER SEVEN

THE PATH OF EVERYDAY LIFE

The believer is the mirror of the believer.
—Muhammad

This chapter and those that follow discuss principles you can use to integrate your experience of money into your spiritual life. Whatever your religious background or spiritual path, these principles can help you unify your personal finances with your spiritual life.

You'll need the courage, diligence, and patience that all spiritual work demands. If you've done the exercises in the preceding chapters, you've already taken some important steps on your path. You've started building the foundation on which you can build further change.

You've begun confronting some deep and powerful attitudes, beliefs, and behavior patterns. You may like some of them and not others. They may produce positive or negative results in your life. The important thing is to see, as clearly as possible, how they structure your experience of what happens to you. You should be able to see how important they are to the way you think, feel, and function in the world.

To the extent that you're seeing how you structure your own experience of life, you're beginning to free yourself from the emotional dominance of your past. In the area of money, you should now have more space to use it rationally and appropriately. You've started learning how to understand yourself through observing your behavior with money.

THE PATH OF EVERYDAY LIFE

Your daily life is your temple and your religion.
—Kahlil Gibran

Ultimately, there's only one spiritual path. All spiritual traditions tell us to look into ourselves, that the goal is within us, "as close as our jugular vein" (Qur'an 50:16). We can learn to see into ourselves as we think, feel, act, and react throughout the day. Everything we do can become a mirror in which we see ourselves more clearly.

Each interaction with family, friends, co-workers, and even strangers becomes a mirror that reflects our attitudes, beliefs, fears, and strengths. As we continue watching, we start seeing why we have these particular characteristics, and we start freeing ourselves of their restrictions. We have an opening to think, feel, and be more conscious.

We have to care deeply and know how to look into ourselves. The depth of our sincerity and the intensity of our concern are the fuel for this process. If we're sincere, objective, and honest with ourselves, we can't fail in this process. Seeing into ourselves is like any other skill: we get better with practice, and we can learn from people who have more experience.

There's a traditional folk tale about Jesus. One day, as he walked by a small village, he felt thirsty. He went over to a well, where a woman was drawing water. He asked if she would pass him a cup to drink from. Recognizing him, she protested, "I'm not important—I'm the village prostitute. You should have someone of greater purity give you what you want." Jesus looked at her with great compassion, saying,

"Daughter, I did not ask for your life story. I only want a drink of water."

This story works on different levels. To some of us, it speaks of the social philosophy that all of us are truly equal and that class or circumstances are not important. To others, it speaks of compassion for those worse off than ourselves. It also illustrates the function of a loving heart. On a deeper level, however, the story tells us about being here now, in the moment.

The woman brought her history with her to the interaction. She acted out her knowledge of her social role and the circumstances she had been living. Jesus was in the moment. All he wanted was a drink of water. He showed her through a simple action being in the present—that the past disappears. We re-create the past in each new moment by our beliefs, thoughts, and actions. This realization is a wonderful clue to the nature of the path to knowledge of the Divine.

NOWHERE TO RUN TO

Who can separate his faith from his actions, or his belief from his occupations? Who can spread his hours before him, saying, "This for God and this for myself; this for my soul, and this other for my body?"

—Kahlil Gibran

If the path to spiritual awareness is self-knowledge, we don't have to go anywhere to find it. We're inside ourselves right now. How could we be anywhere else? We don't have to meet anyone special, or read the right books, or do the right rituals. We just have to look.

Of course, it's a little more complex than that. Looking is fine, but we have to *see*. We're creatures of habit, and we're asleep most of the time, so stepping outside our normal lives, meeting someone, reading something, or practicing looking can be very valuable. Seeing ourselves is a skill like any other: we get better with practice.

Most spiritual traditions are really educational systems for seeing into ourselves. They're maps of inner space, often dressed up in language and imagery that conceal this vital function. Properly understood, they give us a context within which we can learn to see. They help us free ourselves of the habitual, patterned perceptions that have dominated our lives, and they bring us to greater consciousness.

It's like waking up in the morning. We're immediately more aware of our environment. Nothing out there has changed, but we have, and everything is different.

Awareness exercises can help us progress more rapidly. Concentration, meditation, breathing, chanting, and movement techniques can enhance our capacity to see into ourselves nonjudgmentally. These exercises work the same way physical ones do. Repetition, diligence, and proper technique produce success in time. If we want to strengthen our inner awareness, we can put ourselves on a training program that will help us reach our goal, the same way a runner would train for a marathon.

These exercises can help us see the deep roots of our habitual and patterned behavior. The act of seeing, from the neutral space these exercises help us create, helps to free us from having to react or behave as we have been. Change then happens automatically. This is inner freedom.

We have a chance to grow spiritually each moment we're alive. John Lennon once commented that life is what happens while you're making other plans. In each moment, we're thinking, feeling, and reacting to what's happening and to what our minds are doing. The lessons for us to learn are contained in our own being and behavior.

NOWHERE TO HIDE

A man with outward courage dares to die;
A man with inward courage dares to live.
—Lao Tzu

A lot of who we are and the way we behave is based on avoiding pain. In childhood we learned what to think and how to act to get what we wanted from the adults around us. Sometimes our strategies worked, and sometimes they didn't. Sometimes we got the love we wanted or felt safe and secure, and sometimes we didn't.

We modified and refined our strategies according to how well they worked. We built elaborate personality structures and behavior patterns based on the extent to which we succeeded or failed in our efforts to get what we wanted. We made ourselves into the people we are today partially as a response to our childhood environment.

This doesn't make us a victim, although we may have been victimized. We were not passive in this process. We took action, even if it was simply to protect ourselves. We had power, and we used it, regardless of how successful we were. We survived, because we're here now. And while we may not particularly like the person our childhood caused us to become, we should understand that we did what we did to survive whatever happened to us.

We can change many of the beliefs and attitudes we adopted then. We can free ourselves of the behavior patterns and emotional barriers we created. And we can go entirely beyond the level of the personality to experience the Divine Presence.

As we grew up, and as adults, we've continued manipulating the people, places, and things around us. Manipulation in this sense isn't evil or negative. It's an effort to rearrange things to have the pleasure of getting what we want and to avoid the pain of not getting what we want, or of getting what we don't want.

We can't reduce the meaning of life to seeking pleasure and avoiding pain, of course. There's more to human beings than that. At the level of our personality that this occurs, however, it has a lot of validity.

PAINFUL TEACHING

The first three of Buddha's Four Noble Truths are "Life is suffering. The root of suffering is desire. There is a way out." (The fourth is The Eightfold Path, the way out of suffering.) We all have a great deal of pain underneath our attitudes, beliefs, and behavior. Much of it is outside our normal awareness. We're aware of it only peripherally, but that's enough to stimulate us to do whatever we must to avoid it. We may have made ourselves into certain kinds of people, we may behave in certain ways or not behave in other ways to avoid our pain. But all of the great spiritual paths and teachers tell us this spiritual truth: The first step on the path is to stop avoiding ourselves.

The pain that lies at the root of much of our behavior can be our greatest teacher. It can be our guide to the specific personal and spiritual barriers we must overcome to experience the Divine Presence in our lives.

When someone we care about says nice things to us, we feel good. When they say things we don't like, we feel pain. This pain comes from inside us, signaling that there's something we need or want to avoid feeling. The outside events trigger the response: pleasure or pain. In either case, it is our inner structures that determine how we feel.

WATCH CLOSELY

If we can watch ourselves closely enough, if we can encounter our pain and experience it without trying to avoid it, we can be rid of it. And when the pain goes away, it's replaced by the joy of freedom and the potential for experience of the Absolute.

Watch for the things you do to avoid inner pain. That pain may involve specific situations, or it may be a fear of what might happen if you don't act a certain way. You may have made yourself into a certain kind of person or learned certain behaviors to avoid feeling that particular kind of pain.

Eric is a solitary man. Even as a child, he was self-contained and independent. His parents were intellectual and emotionally unexpressive, but they did the best they could and expressed their love in ways they were comfortable with.

Eric quickly learned not to expect much direct emotional nurturance. It was a painful lesson for a little boy, and he reacted by building walls around himself. He became independent and self-contained, both to win his parents' approval and to avoid the pain of being hurt by others who he feared wouldn't give him what he wanted.

Eric still needs love, of course, but it's difficult to find. His self-containment cuts him off from others and makes them feel he's distant and unattached. Eric has become aware of his patterns and has started therapy and daily meditation.

He says, "I watch myself being independent: not needing anyone, enjoying being alone, being this strong person. Sometimes I feel the pain underneath it all. I don't like it. I feel so childish and vulnerable when I feel that way. I do a lot in my life to avoid feeling like that."

Eric is learning to stop avoiding that pain. The more he experiences it, the more he sees where it came from. The more he sees where it came from, the less it affects him. The less his pain affects him, the more free he is to love and receive others' love.

PAIN ISN'T PERMANENT

Confronting our pain doesn't mean we should wallow in it. As our pain arises, we simply feel it, allowing it to be there, like a wave washing up on a beach. Like the wave, the pain will recede in time. Let it go. Another wave bringing pain or happiness will come soon. Let it come. It, too, will recede. When we try to hang on to whatever we're feeling, we're hindering the flow of life.

Start identifying with the one who is experiencing the pain, not the pain itself. You're the beach, not the waves. You can see the wave forming, hear it rushing toward you, feel it crash on the beach, smell the foam and spray. You can feel the pressure of the water as it washes up and the pull as it washes away and tries to take you with it. You don't have to go. You don't have to be pulled into the ocean of temporary experience. You're the beach; you're permanent.

POLISHING THE MONEY MIRROR

By now you have begun to see how important money is in our lives. The more important any aspect of our lives, the more deeply we can see ourselves in relation to it. Like relationships, money can be a powerful tool for experiencing ourselves. It's not the only one, of course, but we need all the tools we can get!

The ideal (seeker) is one who if required to live poorly can so live, and no sense of want will affect him or interfere with the full inner play of the divine consciousness. If he is required to live richly, he can so live and never for a moment fall into desire or attachment to his wealth or to the things he uses, or servitude to self-indulgence. . . .

—Sri Aurobindo

EXERCISES

The following exercises will help you use money as a mirror. Each time you try to see yourself, you're polishing the mirror. You're helping yourself see more and more clearly. The most important things to remember are objectivity and intensity. You have to care deeply and watch without self-judgment.

If you've started a money journal, you can add these exercises to it. You may find that they improve your financial situation as well!

1. If you haven't already tracked your spending for a month, start now. Write down every penny you spend and on what. Watch for the patterns of feeling associated with spending— or deciding not to spend—money.

These emotional patterns are like musical chords, first heard faintly in the background. As you pay attention to them, they become easier to hear and soon you can determine single notes. When you know where each note comes from, you've mastered the exercise.

2. If you don't have a monthly budget, create one now. Look at your expenses and create a model month. Build into it the necessary sums for non-monthly expenses, like automobile insurance. Note your feelings as you go through this exercise. Do you feel nervous, anxious, powerful, in control, controlled, surprised, hopeful, hopeless, and so on? Watch your feelings arise, without judging them. Where do they come from? Why do you feel this way?

3. Your budget should include saving for your personal

financial goals. If you're already saving by contributing to a tax-deferred pension plan, look at your pay stubs or the checks you've written. How does this saving make you feel?

If you're not saving any more than automatic payments to your pension, start saving more, even if it's very little. Save five pounds a month if that's all you can afford. Each time you save, write this sentence ten times in your money journal: "A part of all I earn is mine to keep."

How does saving for the future make you feel? Why do you feel this way? If you haven't been saving, what feelings and beliefs have been associated with that?

4. Start your personal financial plan. Write down a list of specific financial goals you want to achieve. These might include retirement, children's education, or purchasing a house or car.

Calculate how much money will it take to achieve each goal. If you don't know how to do this, a financial adviser can help. There are computer programs that will do this for you as well. To perform the calculation, you'll have to set a time frame for each goal. When you've done this, you'll know how much money you'll need and when you'll need it. You'll know exactly how much you have to set aside each month or year to reach the goals you've chosen, and how much you can spend on yourself now. How does making your goals this detailed make you feel? Why do you feel this way?

5. Add up your resources. Fill out a balance sheet or a personal financial statement. List everything you own and your debts. Your net worth is the value of what you own minus what you owe. Now consider your nonfinancial resources:

you, your skills, your friendships, the people you know, and so forth. How can these help you reach your goals?

6. Start learning about financial planning and investing. These are survival skills in modern society, and there are lots of resources out there to help. There are books, tape courses, classes, seminars, and the like. Observe your feelings as you start learning. What comes up? How do you feel? Where does it come from?

7. If you're not giving money to charitable causes, start doing so. Giving money is an important affirmation of your connection to the Divine Presence. It also affirms your possession of a surplus over your real needs and thus reminds you what your real needs are. Set a monthly or annual amount, and give that regularly.

Try to make your giving as direct as possible. Mailing checks to organizations is the least direct way, and giving money directly to the ultimate recipients is the most direct form of giving. Observe your feelings as you give, regardless of how direct it is.

Try to make your giving as meaningful as possible. You can learn a lot about yourself, considering the difference between giving to a cause you believe in and giving to individuals to help them survive or get back on their feet. Notice the kinds of giving you're attracted to and why you're attracted to them.

Giving your time and energy is more direct than giving money. If you're already giving this way, give some money as well. If you're already giving money, do some direct charitable work.

115

CHAPTER EIGHT

THE AMOUNT YOU HAVE ISN'T IMPORTANT

*The truth will set you free, not because it will give you expla-
nations, but because the conscious experience of the truth . . .
is itself space and light and contact with a higher world.*
—Jacob Needleman

We can have everything we want and still *be* nothing. We
can work and live for the future and still feel empty and
unfulfilled. If we've committed ourselves to the Path of
Everyday Life, if we're playing the game of self-awareness,
there's only one time to do it: *now*.

Our thoughts of the future are fantasy images generated
by our minds. They distract us from perceiving what's happening in this moment. Many people are never in the
moment. They're always someplace else—or "somewhen"
else—planning, thinking, worrying, trying to make sure
things work out the way they want them to.

The next time you're late for something and you find
yourself hurrying along—your mind out ahead of you, worrying about what will happen when you arrive—you'll be
experiencing this phenomenon. Many people do this constantly, to one degree or another.

Richard was living in a spiritual community. He typically
walked around lost in thought. Whenever the community's
leader saw him this way, he'd yell at the top of his voice:
"Richard—stop thinking!" The leader would yell when others

were around, or in the middle of a seminar, or in public places. It didn't matter to him. Richard, however, was very shaken.

"At first I was very embarrassed," Richard says. "After all, there were people around. And I resented being treated that way, being yelled at. What happened was that I stopped thinking so much. I didn't want to be yelled at anymore! I became more present, and as I did I felt more calm and centered. Nothing in my life changed—but *I* did."

Richard was lucky enough to have someone who could administer appropriate and loving shocks to help him learn. He's experienced something new in himself, simply because he lowered his level of internal noise. We don't have to search for spirituality. We simply have to stop avoiding it.

Waiting for More Dough

Waiting until we have more money before we start using our finances as a tool for self-awareness is a wonderful way to procrastinate. How much will be enough? How long will we wait?

If we look closely at this urge, we often find that it's either a result of simple laziness or of wanting to avoid the pain of looking at certain parts of our personalities. Another manifestation of this is the "wishful thinking" syndrome.

Most people daydream about nice things happening. When this filters into the financial realm, however, people can become powerless in the present. There are people who spend a significant part of their income on various lotteries or other forms of gambling. Others chase wild schemes that have little chance of success. Their wishful thinking costs them a lot!

Other people believe that the entire economy is rigged, that everyone in business, banking, investing, and government is crooked and corrupt, and thus there's no hope of success. Each negative news story confirms their point of view. They tend to find something wrong, or something that could go wrong, with everything. Their level of worry is so profound that they seem to exist in a world of negative possibilities. Being in the present moment is impossible in a situation like this.

THE MIRROR'S SIZE DOESN'T MATTER

The size of our mirror is unimportant. It's the strength of the light that helps us see. The light is our awareness, the intensity of our desire to see more clearly. In a strong light, even a sliver of glass will do. Without any light, we're in the dark, despite a wall of mirrors in front of us.

This is why you can and must start now, with what you have. Start with the time you have, with the situation in which you find yourself, and with the money you have. They are the mirror, you are the light.

If the opposite were true, only those with a lot of money and supportive circumstances could grow in awareness. The quest lies within us, and whatever diverts us from that, even for a moment, does us a disservice.

MONEY IS A SACRED TRUST

All wealth belongs to the Divine and those who hold it are trustees, not possessors. It is with them today, tomorrow it may be elsewhere. All depends on the way they discharge their trust while it is with them, in what spirit, with what consciousness in their use of it, to what purpose.
—Sri Aurobindo

We have been entrusted with our wealth, financial and otherwise. As spiritual people, where do we think it came from? How did it get to us? What force was responsible? The

Absolute is the ultimate source of whatever wealth we have.

If our ultimate goal is union with the Absolute, it's more functional to think of ourselves not as owning what we have, but rather as caretakers for the wealth that is temporarily ours.

Remember the biblical parable of the good steward? He made wise use of his master's resources, and his master favored him for it. What are our ultimate resources? They are our time and energy. How do you use yours? What goals do you work toward? The beginning of wisdom in this area is learning to make wise use of the material resources you've been given.

Prudence dictates being able to account for all the money that comes in and goes out. We should be aware of everything we spend, and each expenditure should be a conscious act. This doesn't mean we shouldn't enjoy ourselves. It simply means that our spending should be conscious.

Prudent use of wealth means providing for economic sufficiency. Our basic needs should be satisfied, and we should have excess resources so we can help those who are in need. Wise use of wealth also implies not being possessed by it, that is, not identifying ourselves with what we own. It means not drawing on material consumption and ownership for a sense of identity.

To use our resources appropriately, we should always try to put something away for the future. In our society, without extended families and close-knit communities, this is more important than ever. Each of us must shoulder more of the burden of educating our children, maintaining ourselves in old age, helping our parents, and whatever other long-term goals we may have.

LEARN TO PLAN

We should learn the basic principles and techniques of

personal financial planning. We should understand the time value of money and how compound interest works. We should know some basic financial strategies, including the following:

- how to manage our cash flow
- how to use credit appropriately
- how to use our employee benefits
- how to have the appropriate kinds and levels of insurance protection
- how to invest efficiently and appropriately for the short and the long terms
- how to protect our heirs from estate taxes and the costs of estate administration

We can learn this by reading, taking courses at local community colleges and adult education programs, and going to seminars and workshops.

How Much Is Enough?

You ask, what is the proper limit to a person's wealth? First having what is essential, and second, having what is enough.
—Seneca

One of the most important processes we can experience is deciding what our real material needs are. If we spend our most valuable resource—the time we have in this life—working to fulfill our needs, then we should be very sure we're spending only the appropriate amount of time satisfying them. Any time spent beyond that could have been used for more valuable purposes.

Having only enough doesn't necessarily mean living without everything. We need a certain level of recreation and entertainment. We may need an aesthetically pleasing environment.

Once we understand that real wealth isn't money, but rather a conscious connection with the Absolute, we have the chance to stop feeding our egos with higher and higher levels of consumption. This frees us from an enormous burden of time and energy. Consumption becomes a secondary activity in the process of living.

As we realize this, the entire pattern of our lives can shift. Our reasons for working will be different; the kind of work we do may change as well. Our relationships and the activities we engage in may also shift.

In addition, by consuming only what is essential, we'll be putting less pressure on the economic and ecological systems that support the human race. In this way we connect with people around the world in a responsible rather than an exploitive way.

> *Owning is the entanglement,*
> *wanting is the bewilderment,*
> *taking is the presentiment.*
> *Only he who contains content*
> *remains content.*
> —Lao Tzu

EXERCISES

1. Walk around your home. Look at everything you own. How much of it do you really need? Are there things you need that you don't have? What things do you need, which do you want, and which simply satisfied a somewhat unconscious need at one time and aren't needed anymore?

2. Identify and describe the most important gifts you've ever received, starting from childhood. Identify at least ten. Which have involved physical items, and which have not? Which have been your greatest inner possessions? Which changed your life most significantly? What has your "wealth" consisted of at different times in your life, and what does it consist of now?

3. List your material needs, such as "a color television." List things you have that are in excess of your real needs, such as "the televisions in the basement and bedroom." Other needs might include "a reliable car," but not "two cars" or "a luxury car."

4. Go through each expense in your budget. Which spending is for real needs? How much income would you need for your real needs, to prepare for your future, and to give something to charity?

5. What do you think you should do with the information you've gained in exercises 1-3? Are there ways you could change your life that would make it fit your values better? Are you living above or below the level of "enough"?

If you're below it, what can you do to get there? If you're above it, what can you do to cut back? Are there better uses for the money you now have left over? What are the implications of this for your work and career plans?

A LIFE OF VALUE(S)

If you've worked through the preceding chapters, you should now have a better idea of what really matters to you. The values you've chosen, and the level of income and material existence you really need, can help define your path through this life. The self-knowledge you're gaining will help you free yourself of the patterns of the past and live a more conscious life. The important thing is your commitment to manifest your values and live the life you know you should.

You can't change your whole life—or yourself—overnight. You should start in one area and set meaningful goals you can easily attain. The successes you have will make it easier to keep changing.

You'll experience a sense of meaning that will flow from the harmony between what you're doing and what you believe. The self-knowledge you'll gain will allow a new force into your life. That contact with the Absolute will make you more calm and centered.

You won't be happy all of the time. That's not the point. But as you center yourself in your chosen values and, ultimately, in your connection to the Divine Presence, you'll find yourself less and less affected by the tugs and pulls of what happens to you each moment. You'll find an inner contentment that goes beyond the impact of whatever your immediate experience is.

THE GOLDEN PATH
This is the path from fool's gold to the real thing. It starts inside us, with our most deeply held personal values. We choose our life's goals as a way of expressing these values. Our goals may or may not have a financial component. If they do, we know how to use money to help us get where we're going.

And along the way we know how to use money and other aspects of our lives as a way of seeing into ourselves. As our insight deepens, we gain inner freedom and a more conscious life.

CHAPTER NINE

GOOD WORK

All work is empty save when there is love;
And when you work with love, you bind yourself to
yourself, and to one another, and to God. . . .
Work is love made visible.
—Kahlil Gibran

How we make our money makes a difference. We spend so much time at work, preparing for work, decompressing afterward, and taking vacations to build our strength so we can return to it. Work is in many ways the defining activity of our lives. What we do helps define us to ourselves and to others.

WHAT IS WORK?

For most people, work is a way to convert their time and life energy into money. They use the money to survive, to care for their families, to prepare for the future, and to enjoy themselves.

We have only so much time in our lives. It's our most precious resource. What we do with it is one of the most important issues we'll ever face. Many people find themselves caught in the W2S2 spiral: Work, Work, Spend, Spend.

They work and work to make money, which they spend and spend. And when they spend more than they're currently earning, they're pledging future work to pay their debt.

Working becomes a means to an end rather than an end in itself.

The baby boom generation is the most caught up in the W2S2 trap. For many boomers, freedom from work—having more time—is becoming the ultimate status symbol. There are two basic ways to get that time.

The first is to earn enough money so that at some point in the future we can live on the income from it. This is financial independence. We have stepped off the "work work" wheel.

The second is to lower our needs so that we need less and less income and thus have to work less and less. We can adopt more flexible work patterns, work at different things, and have more time.

If we combine the two methods, it's possible to become financially independent earlier than we might think.

It's important to consider whether financial independence is really a good idea. Work engages us with the world in personal, social, and spiritual ways. Opting out of this can be a form of withdrawal: *If the game can't be the way I want it to, I'll take my ball and go home.*

People often find that when they don't have to work, they suffer a crisis of meaning. When there's nothing we have to do, we tend not to *want* to do anything. At this point, you may be saying to yourself, "I'd sure like to try that for a while!" And you might enjoy it—for a while. Consider the following story:

A woman died and found herself in a beautiful white room. As she sat there, somewhat confused, a man walked in, wearing a beautiful flowing robe. "Congratulations! You've arrived!" he said. "Is there anything you'd like? You can have anything you want here, any pleasure, whatever you desire."

The woman thought for a while and told the man her desires. He opened a door for her, and walking through it, she saw the way she would satisfy the first desire she had mentioned.

Some time later, she returned to the first room and waited for the man to arrive. When he came in, she went over to him, saying, "I've done everything I wanted, twice. I've done things I didn't want to do, just to do something. I'm tired of it. But I know what will solve my problem. Do you have some work for me to do?"

"Oh no," the man replied. "That's the one thing we don't allow here. No one is allowed to work."

"What?" the woman asked. "If I can't work, I might as well be in Hell."

"But where did you think you were?" replied the man.

Of course, it is possible to find meaningful things to do besides working for a living! If we choose that path, we're accepting the responsibility of finding meaningful activities. It takes creativity, but it certainly can be done.

Good Work

As chapter one noted, E. F. Schumacher suggests that work has three purposes:

1. To provide necessary and useful goods and services.
2. To enable us to use and thereby perfect our gifts like good stewards.
3. To engage in this work in service to and in cooperation with others, which helps liberate us from our inborn egocentricity.*

---

*E. F. Schumacher, *Good Work* (New York: Harper & Row, 1979), 3-4.

THE FIRST GOOD

So many of the goods and services we produce have no *real* use! It's important to know that what we're working at is important to others. How we define "necessary and useful" will depend on our personal growth and spiritual insight.

THE SECOND GOOD

We're stewards of our personal gifts as well as of our material ones. We have an obligation to use, develop, and perfect them. In so doing, we develop and perfect ourselves. Work is one of the most important arenas in which we can discharge this obligation.

There used to be a sense of craftsmanship in many occupations. Most people aren't involved in the direct manufacture of things anymore, but the idea of craftsmanship has a lot to offer us in learning to deal with the world of work. The concept of work as a craft implies a lifetime spent learning to master something. People learn diligence, patience, and self-discipline as well as whatever specific skills are necessary. There was also an element of having been "called" to the work, which gives the worker's experience an added dimension.

THE THIRD GOOD

Human beings are social animals. We exist in groups from the moment of birth. Work offers us a way to be with others, to make meaningful efforts together. The world of work has its own culture, one of interactions with others and rules of behavior. Participating in this culture helps reduce our natural egocentricity. To work well, we have to get along with others.

WORK IS A SCHOOL OF BECOMING

The method of gaining your livelihood must not . . .
increase the paranoia and separateness of the world. . . .

Good Work

*Suitable right livelihood for any specific individual is
determined by the totality of forces acting upon him.*
—Ram Dass

Three stonecutters worked side by side in a quarry. Day in and day out, they cut blocks of stone, which were hauled away for use in construction. One day two women, a teacher and a student, came to visit the workers. "Do you know what they're doing?" asked the teacher. "They're cutting stone," the student answered.

"Perhaps you should ask them," the teacher replied. So the student did. "I'm cutting stone blocks, each one exactly alike, so I can get paid," the first one answered. "I'm cutting stone blocks so I can earn a living for my family," said the second one. The third stonecutter answered, "I'm creating homes for people to live in, beautiful walls and archways for their villages, and churches for them to worship in."

The teacher turned to the student, asking, "Which one of these men is right?"

This story helps us see what function a sense of purpose can serve in the world of work. Although we may be doing exactly what others do, we can use our work as a way of serving others. We do people a service by producing goods or services that satisfy their needs. Our interpretation of "needs" and what is "useful and necessary" is up to us.

If we bake bread for people or sell bread to them, we're helping them nourish themselves so they can be renewed and live their lives. We're also giving them the chance to share food with family and friends and to enjoy the love and friendship that these interactions provide.

The spirit with which we work is passed along to those who consume what we produce or who use our services. If we work with indifference, if we begrudge our labor, if we don't love what we do, then we're fruitlessly engaged regardless of the quality of the product. And whether or not we actually meet them, the spirit with which we work is passed along to the ultimate consumers.

Work offers us the chance to engage ourselves fruitfully, to become simultaneously more and less than we were. If we settle for less than that, we're not using the talents we've been given. We're not being a good steward of our wealth. And we're not taking advantage of one of life's great opportunities for spiritual growth.

We might find ourselves changing the work we do, or we might change the way we do our current work. It's doing good work that counts, not finding something new and different that excites us in a way our old work didn't.

LABOR-SAVING DEVICES

At the dawn of the industrial age, we began developing machines that could do the work of hundreds of people. This trend has continued, and now machines do the work of millions of people. Social scientists, commentators, and science fiction writers used this trend to try to predict the future. They saw a time of great leisure for the human race, when machines would do all the work. They thought it would be a time of flowering human creativity. Science fiction written as late as the 1950s involved these kinds of scenarios.

Of course, this hasn't happened, nor is it likely. Exactly the opposite has occurred. It's one of the great contradictions of our era. Despite an incredible array of tools, machines, and technological processes devoted to saving time, people have less time than ever before. People in modern industrial societies are more pressed for time and thus more cut off from directly experiencing the natural environment, each other, and themselves.

This increased psychological pressure has generated an increased interest in religion and mysticism, particularly the more emotional and fundamentalist varieties; increased use of alcohol and other drugs; greater emphasis on recreational sex; children becoming sexually active earlier; more violence; an increased pace of leisure activities; and more reliance on television for entertainment.

We're trying to fill our inner emptiness, to reconnect with an experience that would seem real to us. Each year we find more powerful ways to stimulate strong emotions, such as sexually explicit television and movies, sports that push us to the limit, parachuting from planes, or jumping off tall structures with elastic cords attached to us.

Technological progress often seems to cause more work rather than less, and the stress of change demands more and more of our energies. Schumacher suggests that the amount of genuine leisure in a society is generally in inverse proportion to the amount of labor-saving machinery it possesses.[*]

The reason for this is simple. It's the Buddha's First Noble Truth: "The cause of suffering is desire." The more we can produce, the more wants we can satisfy. The more wants we can satisfy, the more we want. *Wants are endless. Humans are insatiable.*

We'll never catch up by finally discovering the great technological breakthrough that solves all our problems. Whatever we develop will create its own new set of wants.

This isn't an argument for giving up on technology. It doesn't mean we should all return to a rural, agricultural way of life. That's obviously impossible. But the more we see how technology affects us, the more we can wisely direct the kinds of technology we develop.

[*] E. F. Schumacher, *Good Work*, 25.

THE STRAIN OF STRAIN

Modern life has substituted mental strain for physical strain. We once thought this was an advantage. Physical labor was our past, it was society in a lower form, and it was more crude. In a society that highly valued its intellectual progress, physical labor was often viewed with mild contempt.

Now we find that a life that demands great and constant mental effort drains us of the energy we need to stay attuned to the Divine Presence in our daily lives. The level of nervous strain the average person experiences would have been thought cruel punishment in the past.

This is one reason for the frantic pace at which people play. "Work hard and play hard," say the television commercials. If you do everything hard, where's your attention? Where is life's ease and grace? We call play "recreation." True recreation comes not from doing something else just as hard, but from a change in the quality of our efforts—perhaps from not doing anything or from doing something playfully.

We need a lot of energy and the capacity to focus it to go through our day fully aware of our internal processes and of what's occurring around us. If our work takes all our energy, there's none left over for the internal work. Freeing ourselves from our habitual patterns of belief and behavior with money gives us more energy for the Path of Everyday Life.

If we're serious about achieving inner freedom, we'll consider the work patterns we've adopted. How much energy do they demand of us? Is our work an expression of our personal values? What sorts of relationships with others does our work involve us in? Do we produce something that's necessary and useful? Is our work, as Kahlil Gibran said, "love made visible"?

132

Good Work

Write your answers to the following questions. Answer as honestly and completely as possible, but without self-judgment or condemnation.

1. How do you feel about your work? What do you like and dislike about it? Is your work "love made visible"? Why or why not? Be as precise as possible. If your work doesn't fit that description, can you think of ways to make it fit?

2. What kinds of relationships and interactions with others do you have at work? Are they fulfilling, positive, and supportive? Are they threatening and negative? Do they undermine you in various ways? Are there ways you could change them and make them more positive?

3. Look at your list of personal values. Is your work an expression of these values? Does it conflict with them? Describe the connection between your work and each of your top five or ten values. If there isn't such a connection, what could you do to create one?

4. Consider yourself as someone with skills rather than as someone in a specific role. These skills may involve people, ideas and data, or tools and equipment. Think back over all the jobs you've had, all the hobbies you've enjoyed, and what you've done for fun. What skills were you using when you were happy and fulfilled by these activities?*

What Color Is Your Parachute? A Practical Manual for Job Hunters and Career Changers, by Richard B. Bolles, offers a series of excellent exercises for people who want to shift gears in life and find more meaningful work.

5. Take some time, make yourself comfortable, and daydream the perfect work for you. Forget what's realistic or what you think is possible. Just relax and let your subconscious generate images.

Don't reject anything, regardless of how silly it seems. Don't become attached to any particular image, no matter how attractive. Just let the images come and go. It's like shifting your conscious mind into neutral, while remaining focused on the problem. Daydreaming this way may not be easy for you. Practice will change that.

6. If daydreaming doesn't produce positive results, you can try this technique to gain some insight. You can also use this to flesh out an image you've gotten while daydreaming. Imagine yourself in the perfect job. Put yourself into the image you saw in your daydream, or create one in your mind. The following questions will help you make your image more real:

- What would you be feeling and thinking?
- What would you hear, see, taste, and smell?
- What kind of surroundings would you work in?
- What kind of people would be around you, and how would you relate to them?
- Would you be working primarily with people, data, or equipment?
- How would other people think of you?
- How would your work be necessary and useful?
- How would this work relate to your personal values?

7. What steps would you have to take to start doing the kind of work you imagined in exercises 5 and 6? How

Good Work

long would those steps take? What could you do in the next
month to start the process? The next six months? The next
year?

8. If your current work could become good work for
you, list the things you could do to make it that way. How
long would each of them take? What intermediate steps
would they require? What could you do tomorrow to take
the first step?

135

CHAPTER TEN

ACCEPTANCE: THE PATH OF GRATITUDE, SURRENDER, AND JOY

Much of this book has focused on gaining self-knowledge and freeing yourself from the constraints of childhood behavior patterns. You've started making conscious choices about your personal values and how you want to live. You've begun choosing your personal values and researching what good work might be for you.

You've started using your daily life as a mirror. You may now see yourself more clearly. You're better able to see your beliefs and behavior patterns in what happens to you each moment. You've accomplished a lot! You're ready for the next step.

SEND AN OPEN INVITATION

Let life ripen and then fall;
Will is not the way at all.
—Lao Tzu

We can't force the Divine Presence to enter our lives. We can't *make* it happen, but we can *let* it happen. As we free ourselves from the past, we create an inner space in which we can recognize the Absolute in ourselves. As we create this calm center, we automatically contact the deep spirituality that is the birthright of every human being, regardless of culture, time, socioeconomic standing, or religious tradition. Here's how we can help this process along.

IT'S NOT *OUR* WILL

What's the ultimate source of the results of our efforts? We work hard to achieve things in the world. We try to have certain kinds of relationships, try to be certain kinds of people, try to achieve our goals at work, and so forth.

We look to the future and judge the present by how well things have worked out. Did we get what we wanted? Did things work out right? If so, we're happy. If not, we're sad, angry, depressed, or determined to do better. Regardless of the specific emotion, our emotional state usually depends on how things work out. We're enslaved by externals.

If we're leading a spiritual life, our efforts aren't the true cause of what we receive. Whatever we receive as the result of what we're trying to achieve—good or bad, positive or negative—is a gift from the Divine Presence.

Whatever wealth we have—power, fame, possessions, friends, opportunities, talents, or abilities—is a gift we've received. Whatever problems we have—limitations, challenges, crises, losses, and pain—are also gifts. They come to us through the action of divine grace, acting through ourselves, other people, and circumstances.

We receive financial gifts every day. Income from work, return on investments, or profits from business come to us. We may also receive losses, of course. God doesn't guarantee us constant financial gain.

IT MAY BE MORE BLESSED TO GIVE, BUT IT'S HARDER TO RECEIVE

All these results, whether positive or negative, can be blessings to the seeker. Each gift offers us an opportunity to experience gratitude. Gratitude is an emotional key that can open the door so the Absolute can enter our lives. As we reject the egocentric, spiritually arrogant, and ignorant belief that our actions dominate our lives, we affirm our openness to the Absolute.

Disgusted with his life, a young man decided to live spiritually. He became a beggar, asking for money on a street corner every day. His approach was "Spare change for a seeker?"

He felt superior to the people who passed and even to those who gave him money. They seemed so caught up in their lives—their jobs, their work, their fears. He could see all of it in their faces. He was glad to be out of that life-style.

One day a well-dressed man walked by. Looking searchingly at the beggar, he walked up, and instead of putting money in the young man's cup, he took the money from the cup and walked away.

Shocked, the young man ran after him. "Wait! That's mine! You're stealing it! I need it!" he cried. The well-dressed man stopped. "You can have it back if you wish," he said, dropping it at the younger man's feet. "It will do you no good. Your contempt for those who gave it to you makes their gifts worthless to you. You could have so much more, if you wished."

The young man reached for the money, fully intending to take it and return to his begging. As he bent down, however, his foolish arrogance became clear to him. He stood and humbly asked his companion for help.

"Now you can receive," the man said. "Come to my office at 9:00 A.M. tomorrow. Oh, yes, wear a suit. You're my new assistant."

Receiving well is very difficult. Giving is much easier. In addition to whatever pleasure you feel, giving can involve a feeling of being "one up" on the recipient. It's easier to do something that makes you feel superior, even if it's just because of superior material circumstances. Receiving often brings with it the burden of gratitude and the desire to "even things up." If that isn't possible, the recipient can feel diminished by the gift.

SPIRITUALITY IS EVERY MOMENT

Gratitude opens us to the Absolute because it keeps us from believing that we're the center of the universe. If we believe that we personally are the source of everything in our lives, we've set ourselves up as God's equals. This creates an inner barrier that prevents us from experiencing our connection with the Divine Presence.

We can lower that barrier by being grateful for everything we receive. We can be grateful for the big things, the little things, and just for being alive each moment. Our gratitude opens a space for a new force to enter our experience.

When we can accept, deeply and completely, that the results of our actions are gifts from the Absolute, we experience humility and spiritual truth. These are the opposites of arrogance and ignorance, and they transform us in important ways.

EXERCISES: ADOPTING AN ATTITUDE OF GRATITUDE

1. Practice being grateful for all the money you receive, whether through work, investments, or gifts from others.

- Each time you receive a payment, such as a paycheck, a dividend, a capital gain, or a gift, write down the benefits you'll receive from this money. What will it let you do—pay your bills (have electricity for the many things you use it for), pay your mortgage (live in your home), eat good food (share it with others), clothe yourself, prepare for the future, share with those who have less? What emotional benefits have you received as a result of these things?

- Write down what others had to do to help you receive these funds. How many people had to come to work with you, earn money to purchase what you produce, and so forth? How many people had to cooperate for you to have the opportunity to invest in a certificate of deposit, stock, bond, or government security?

  Who raised these people and educated them? Who cares for their health? Who pays taxes for police and fire protection for them? Who provides these services?

2. Review your monthly budget. Be grateful for each expenditure and what you received in the process.

- How many people had to act so you could make each purchase? How many people did it take to produce what you bought, market it, and transport it to the store? How many people made the materials out of which your purchase was created? How many others helped design the production and marketing processes? Continue as in the preceding exercise.

3. Practice being grateful as you pay your taxes and your bills. Regardless of your opinion of government waste and other political considerations, remember that your taxes provide many services you need. Your bills offer you another chance to practice gratitude. You may pay for electricity, gas, water, fuel oil, and telephone service. How many people have to work to bring these services to your house?

4. When you can be grateful for the material gifts you receive, start being grateful for your capabilities and talents. If you're a good athlete, a good musician, capable at math, good with people—whatever your abilities are—you

can be grateful for them. They were given to you, after all.

5. Say thank-you more often. Practice thanking people more. Thank your friends for their friendship and your loved ones for their love. Thank your co-workers for their cooperation and those who oversee your work for their supervision. Even if what others do doesn't always help your efforts, or even if they obstruct you, you can be grateful for their obstruction.

In some warrior traditions, we find the concept of the "worthy opponent." This is someone whose skills are equal to or greater than your own, whom you can test yourself against. The struggle gives you the opportunity to go beyond yourself, to reach new levels of skill. This concept survives today in athletic rivalries, whether between teams or individuals.

When basketball great Larry Bird announced his retirement from active play with the Boston Celtics, an interviewer asked Magic Johnson how he felt. Magic had battled against Bird in some memorable games and hadn't yet announced his own retirement. He expressed a profound sense of loss. "Everyone in the NBA [National Basketball Association] is competitive," he said, "or else they wouldn't be here. But some players keep you up at night. Some guys are so good they force you to raise your game to a different level. That's what Larry did for me. I'll miss him."

6. When you give money, things, or time, be grateful for the opportunity and for having a surplus above your needs. Give in gratitude and accept others' gratitude. Experience the connection that gratitude can create between giver and recipient, rather than the separation of "one-upmanship."

7. Be grateful for your troubles, afflictions, and problems. When people obstruct you or hurt you, they're giving you an opportunity to transcend your pain and self-imposed limitations. You might not be grateful to them, but rather to God for the opportunity to grow.

In Alcoholics Anonymous, the original Twelve Step program, gratitude plays a very important role. Recovering alcoholics often call themselves "grateful alcoholics," not just because they've sobered up, but also because the disease of alcoholism itself presented them with an opportunity to embrace a spiritual journey and come into contact with a Higher Power.

THE NEXT STEP: SURRENDER

Don't worry, be happy.
—Meher Baba

Experiencing gratitude can open an inner door for us. The more grateful we become for everything we've been given, the easier it is to surrender control. When we accept, profoundly and completely, that the results of our actions are out of our hands, we can relax and stop trying to control the outcomes of our efforts.

Trying to control things, trying to make them come out the way we want them to, is based on the supposition that our efforts cause things to happen in the first place. When we learn to accept that this isn't the case, we can let go of our emotional attachment to the results of our actions. This is surrender.

Our inner state—whether we are happy or sad, elated or depressed—is based on how things go for us. If we've had a good day, we feel happy. If things haven't gone our way, we feel sad, depressed, angry, alienated, and so forth.

This attachment to having things work our own way demands an incredible amount of emotional energy. First, we have to pay attention constantly to the results of our actions. We have to scrutinize everything that happens and compare it to what we wanted: *Is this good? Is it what I wanted? Can I use it to get more of what I want? Can I avoid being hurt or feeling pain?*

This goes on constantly throughout the day. The extent to which we worry about the future is related to the amount of control we still have to surrender.

When things don't go our way, our anger, sadness, or depression takes energy. Even if things do go our way, happiness takes energy and always brings with it the realization that it is only temporary, that in an instant things can change.

We can save all this energy by giving up our emotional attachment to the results of our actions. Our focus can then shift to the quality of the actions themselves and to our moment-to-moment connection with the Divine Presence. This is surrendering.

Gloria owns a small needlepoint shop. She's been practicing gratitude and surrender in her business. "Decisions used to make me crazy," she says. "I'd obsess about them, focus on them night and day. My family would joke about it—'Oh, Mom's got another problem'—but I knew they felt ignored. I was just so worried about how things would turn out."

Gloria started working to develop gratitude. Gradually, her emotional attachment to how things work out weakened. She found herself making decisions differently. "I don't obsess anymore," Gloria says. "I gather the information I need and kind of let it stew. I know the ultimate results are out of my hands. The answer usually comes to me—it just appears, right in front of me. And, you know, a good part of the time, the problems themselves disappear. They weren't things I really had to decide in the first place!"

SURRENDER TO . . .

Those who flow as life flows know
They need no other force.
They feel no wear, they feel no tear,
They need no mending, no repair.
—Lao Tzu

Surrendering doesn't mean becoming passive or fatalistic. We're surrendering to life, that is, to the energy that animates everything, because as we break the emotional attachment to the outcomes of our efforts, we open ourselves to a much greater world of possibilities. When we *let* things happen rather than try to *make* them happen, we unlock a door to a wider range of potential results. And when we're not attached to a particular outcome, we can often see positive aspects in results that would have baffled or even enraged us previously.

We're ultimately surrendering to the Divine Presence. When we get ourselves out of the way, the Absolute can manifest itself more clearly in our lives. And, because we're refocusing our awareness on our connection with the Absolute, we're more in tune with it.

When we're not living in our mental image of how we want our future to be, we can focus on our inner connection with the Absolute. We can use our lives as a mirror and learn more about ourselves and our behavior. Our self-defeating behavior, in all areas of our lives, can change. As we see beyond ourselves, our insight can focus on what lies beyond us: the Divine Presence.

DOES SURRENDER MEAN DEFEAT?

A student once asked a great Sufi what he thought the spiritual path was. The Sufi replied, "The Path is the feeling of joy when sudden disappointment comes." Sudden disappointment can be shocking. Out of nowhere, it seems, our hopes have been dashed. How do we react? With anger, fear, despair? Do we say, "There it goes again—nothing ever works out"? Do we grow more determined to succeed, telling ourselves, "I'll try again tomorrow, but I'll make it work out for me sooner or later"?

We might feel that we didn't deserve to have what we wanted. We might tell ourselves that we didn't *really* care. We might even stop trying altogether to get what we want. All these responses affirm our emotional attachment to the results of our actions.

Why would someone feel joyful at being disappointed? If we were trying to live spiritually, and something disappointing happened, we could tell by our very disappointment that we were attached to the outcome of our efforts. What an opportunity! What joy! We've been given the teaching we need to grow closer to the Divine Presence. We have a priceless opportunity to grow.

The Sufi poet Rumi tells a story about the Prophet Muhammad. One day he was getting ready to put his boots on, and an eagle swooped down and grabbed one from his hand. As the eagle flew away with it, the Prophet stared in surprise. Why had this bird, which would ordinarily take no interest in a human's possessions, taken his boot?

The eagle then dropped the boot from a great height. As it fell, a scorpion slid out of it. Had Muhammad slid his foot into it, he would have been stung and could have died. The eagle flew back to him. "Oh, Prophet!" said the bird. "I would not have interfered with your actions, but I could not let your message be stopped by such a disaster." Muhammad learned in that moment about surrendering to new possibilities.

Comedian and activist Dick Gregory tells a story about the Boston College football team. Some years ago, they were having a perfect season and were one of the best teams in the country. Their last game was against College of the Holy Cross, which hadn't had a good season at all. The Boston College players were confident of a victory. Inviting their friends and family along, they partied at a club the night before the game.

Holy Cross won the game, by a lopsided score. The loss was such a humiliation that the Boston College players couldn't bring themselves to party again. That night, the club they had gone to the night before, and to which they would have returned had they won, burned to the ground. It was one of the worst nightclub disasters in Boston history.

We may never know what disasters may have been avoided by our not getting what we want. Furthermore, getting what we want can also be a disaster, sometimes in ways we won't see for many years. Even so, this truth is not meant to console us in our loss, but rather to help us break our emotional connections to the outcomes of our efforts. Victory or loss, regardless of our initial preference for one over the other, shouldn't affect our moment-to-moment connection with the Absolute, which is what really matters. The worldly struggle is merely the training ground on which we can come to refocus ourselves.

THE WAY OF THE WARRIOR

It seems paradoxical that to walk the warrior's path through life, we must first surrender. Think of great warriors going to battle. They must act courageously to fulfill their destiny. Acting courageously means not being affected by a fear of death, disfigurement, or defeat. To avoid these fears, the warriors must overcome their emotional attachment to results and concentrate completely on the quality of their actions in each moment.

Such was the path of the samurai warriors—or at least those who grasped the essence of what combat had to teach them. If they could give up their fear of losing, break their attachment to staying alive, then they could focus completely on each sword stroke and, in the process, be transformed. They could reach new levels of awareness.

Samurai who found this path often gave up fighting. They started practicing calligraphy, poetry, painting, the tea ceremony, and other arts that let them be warriors of awareness rather than actual fighters.

A traditional Japanese story tells us that a long time ago, a young samurai wandered through the countryside, challenging local swordsmen as he traveled. He defeated them all, for he was very skillful. Hearing of a legendary swordsman who lived far away in the north, the young samurai went in search of him. If he could defeat this living legend, his name, too, would become known throughout Japan.

After years of wandering, the samurai heard that the warrior he sought was at an inn in the next village. He prepared himself, bathing and oiling his hair and putting on his best kimono. He carefully cleaned and sharpened his sword. Then he strode to the inn.

Entering the courtyard, he saw the great warrior. Dirty and unkempt, a small, nondescript man sat noisily slurping rice. His robe was stained, and his sword was so rusted that it could not be drawn from its scabbard.

Despite his disappointment at his opponent's appearance, the young man roared out his challenge, reciting his lineage and recounting his victories. He described his search for a worthy opponent. He invited the warrior to single combat and emphasized his intention to defeat him.

The older man said nothing. He gobbled rice, shoveling it into his mouth with chopsticks as he held the bowl to his lips. Without raising his eyes from his rice bowl, he reached up with the chopsticks, plucked four flies from the air, and laid them in a row on the table in front of him. Then he went back to eating his rice.

The young man stood for a moment in amazement, realizing that he was not even in the same class as this warrior. His pride disappeared. He humbly asked if he could become the man's disciple. Years later his sword, too, was rusted to its scabbard.

The young warrior discovered that he had been fighting the wrong battle. He had struggled for martial skill and the ability to defeat others. The real battle, personified by the older samurai, was the battle with himself. The victory was awareness, not triumph over others.

When we've surrendered our attachment to the outcomes of our actions and how the world should be, we can live without fear. What were we afraid of, anyway, but of getting bad things, of losing, of being humiliated, of being hurt, of not getting what we wanted? When we've given up the emotional attachment to the results, the fear drops away. When we can accept whatever comes and be grateful for it, we can live without fear. The quality of our life changes. We have more physical and mental energy to put into our actions, and the quality of our efforts can improve dramatically.

> *A man is free in proportion to the things*
> *he can afford to let alone.*
> —Henry David Thoreau

STEPS ON THE PATH

There are different levels of surrender. The first, discussed earlier, involves giving up our attachment to outcomes. Our emotional state is no longer intensely dependent on whether or not we get what we want.

As we progress on the path and refocus ourselves on the Divine, we can surrender even more. We can surrender our emotional attachment to our own emotional states. We no longer grasp at happiness and flinch from sadness. We release these emotions and stop inwardly clutching at them.

Happiness and sadness come and go, depending on events, but we don't try to hang on to them and keep them with us. We're not happy about being happy or sad about being sad. We don't despair at despair. Our feelings come and go, like waves on a beach. We're not trying to control the people, places, and things around us to find pleasure and avoid pain.

As we stop identifying with our feelings, our inner state can shift even more. We identify more with whoever is standing on that beach watching the waves. That being, that "I," is our doorway to the Divine. That "I" is our inner connection to consciously experiencing God. To move into that experience, however, we must first stop doing everything we're now doing that diverts us from that awareness. Gratitude and surrender can lead us toward the One.

———

EXERCISES

1. The first exercise for awareness is . . . Be aware. Watch yourself reacting to everything that happens to you. Watch yourself feeling differently as good things and bad things happen. Understand that your particular psychology determines whether an event is good or bad.

The crucial part of this exercise is to let go of your feelings. Don't suppress, resist, or express them. Feel the pleasure when good things happen . . . and let it go. Don't try to hang onto it, to structure your life so you only feel good. Feel the pain when bad things happen . . . and let it go. Don't suppress it or express it by dumping it on someone else. Don't talk yourself out of feeling it . . . feel it, and let it go.

It's as if you were standing on a beach watching the waves wash up on the sand. Each wave hits the beach, flows up a little way, and then flows back to its source. Some waves are larger than others. They wash up farther and stay on the beach longer. All waves eventually recede, however. They must—it's their nature.

You can't stop the waves or keep them from returning to the sea. The more you try, the more you ensure that the same waves will return to your beach over and over. Let your feelings rise and fall, come and go. Feel them, good and bad.

Watch yourself struggling to control your life; to manipulate people, places, and things to get what you want and to feel good; and to avoid what you don't want and to not feel bad. You behave in certain ways so others will be nice to you, and in other ways to avoid actions you'd experience negatively. You do things to avoid feeling lonely, scared, fearful, and so on. This struggle goes on and on, and many people stay trapped in it all their lives.

Spirituality means getting out of this trap and learning to use your life as a spiritual exercise. Your spiritual path, regardless of your religious tradition, is to stop avoiding, suppressing, or dumping your pain on others. Pain, loneliness, fear, anxiety—these are all barriers that stand between you and God. Avoiding them merely strengthens their grip on you. Let these feelings arise—so you can let go of them.

When you can do this, you'll have broken the grip that

these feelings and the events that stimulated them had on you. In that moment, a different consciousness emerges.

2. When you invest money, you can surrender to the possibility inherent in that investment. If you put money in a bank, consider the number of people who work at the bank so you can receive your interest. Consider the people working at all the businesses that borrow from the bank, which enables the bank to pay the interest. If you invest in a stock, consider the number of people who have to work and cooperate for your stock to go up in value. Consider the people who have to help them, the police who protect them, the medical people who help them stay healthy, and so on.

If you invest in a bond, consider the number of people who have to work together so the corporation or municipality can generate enough income to make the interest payment. You can't control all this, so why try? You've done your work in choosing the investment, and you'll monitor its performance. The rest is out of your hands.

A LIFE OF JOY

"Why aren't you dancing with joy this very moment?"
is the only relevant spiritual question.
—Pir Vilayat Khan

Have you ever noticed that the American Declaration of Independence says, "life, liberty, and the *pursuit* of happiness"? The wise framers of our system of government knew that happiness, joy, and contentment come as the results of other things. They're gifts. They just happen.

When we've become grateful for everything we've received and continue to receive, we may find ourselves happy, regardless of our material circumstances. Who wouldn't be happy, constantly receiving gifts from the Divine? The experience feels strange the first few times we have it. There we are, in the midst of our struggles with life. Nothing has changed. We're no richer, thinner, or different, but . . . we're happy.

Gratitude for everything we receive affirms our connection with the source of the gifts. This constant affirmation opens our heart, minds, and spirit. Surrendering, giving up our efforts to control our lives, frees enormous energy. We can then use the energy to enhance the quality of our moment-to-moment efforts. Paradoxically, by giving up our efforts to control the outcomes of what we do, the results often improve beyond anything we had previously imagined.

First gratitude, then surrender, then joy. As we use our experience of money to free ourselves from our patterns of behavior, our hearts open and joy can enter. Men and women in every spiritual tradition have reported an incredible joy that words cannot adequately describe. This is "the peace that passeth all understanding." It comes from direct contact with the Divine Presence. It comes, for whatever reasons, when we have stopped driving it away by our unconscious, habitual patterns of beliefs, attitudes, and behavior.

It was said that soon after his enlightenment, the Buddha passed a traveler on the road who was struck by the extraordinary radiance and peacefulness of the Buddha's presence. The man asked him, "My friend, what are you? Are you a celestial being or a god?"

"No," said the Buddha.

The man then asked, "Well, are you some kind of magician or wizard?" Again the Buddha answered, "No."

The traveler persisted, asking, "Are you a man like me?"
Again the Buddha responded, "No."

"Well, then, what are you?" the traveler asked.

The Buddha replied, "I am awake."*

---

*Christina Feldman and Jack Kornfield, *Stories of the Spirit, Stories of the Heart* (New York: HarperCollins, 1991), 392.

CHAPTER ELEVEN

THE RAZOR'S EDGE:
FAITH REQUIRES ACTION

Faith without prayer is beneficial,
but there is no benefit in prayer without faith.
—Rumi

Faith is believing in something that doesn't exist for us yet. Many people in our rational age find it impossible to have faith. It can seem crazy, even primitive, to believe in something that has no physical existence, that can't be seen, heard, touched, tasted, or smelled. And having faith just because a religious tradition or organization says we should seems unintelligent and phony.

Furthermore, those who've attained conscious knowledge of the Divine tell us that once we know the Divine, faith falls away. Certainty replaces it. So why *should* we have faith? Why do we need it? Is it just for consolation, a crutch for the weak to lean on?

FAITH IS FOR THE STRONG

Thirty spokes are made one by holes in a hub
By vacancies joining them for a wheel's use;
The use of clay in molding pitchers
Comes from the hollow of its absence;

Doors, windows, in a house,
Are used for their emptiness:
Thus we are helped by what is not
To use what is.
—Lao Tzu

The purpose of faith is to motivate us to act. Faith focuses our energies in the proper direction. This is why faith is for the strong, for those committed to changing themselves. Only those with courage and a strong sense of purpose can dedicate themselves to doing the inner work. Faith isn't for God, it's for human beings. Faith isn't something the Divine Presence demands of us, such as that we worship in certain ways, say certain phrases, or adopt particular beliefs.

Faith is an attitude the seeker uses to focus his or her inner energies, to be constantly reminded of life's purpose, and to keep walking the path. This inner work isn't easy. It takes energy and determination, courage and self-discipline. What keeps us going? What keeps us working on ourselves? It's faith—faith that our efforts will result in further change, that we're doing the right thing, that we're on the path to real change.

BELIEF AND UNDERSTANDING

We think of faith as belief without understanding, and we may consider it primitive. But the reverse is just as bad. Understanding without belief leads to the use of knowledge for whatever purpose, regardless of its danger or negative function, just because it's possible. Without faith, science and technology veer off in directions that don't serve the real growth of human beings, but rather enrich the few at the expense of the many.

Faith should serve to focus our intelligence. It should help us live our lives for the highest purpose we can conceive of. We're not describing faith in God here, but faith in the path, faith in the possibility of changing ourselves, faith in—us.

MONEY AND FAITH

As we've seen by now, money is based on faith. The concept of money as a mass psychological agreement, and our willingness to use something as money, depend entirely on our faith that those around us share that agreement and will accept that thing as such.

Saving and investing are also based on faith. We must believe that we have a future and that our investments can succeed. Thus we're willing to reduce our current spending to have more in the future.

Giving money away is an affirmation of faith. We're affirming our belief that we'll survive, that we have enough coming in for our real needs, and that we'll continue to be supported. We're acting on our belief in the abundance of our material blessings.

Working is an affirmation of faith. We believe that those who work with us will come to work and do what they're supposed to do. We believe our employer will succeed, that others will buy or use the goods or services we produce. If we work for a branch of government, we believe the funding for our bureau, agency, or department will continue.

In fact, just living demands a great deal of faith. We believe that others will obey the traffic laws so we can get to work. We believe that the newspaper will be delivered, that there will be electricity when we wake up, and lots more. We already have a great deal of faith!

THE PATH OF THE PATH

Hypocrisy is the gap between belief and behavior. It's not simply saying things we don't believe, behaving in ways that conflict with cherished personal values, or not acting on the basis of what we believe.

Faith—in the possibility of change, in the process, in the goal—requires action; otherwise we experience the gap of hypocrisy. Once we act, however, we begin to see the process of change at work. Our actions have produced results that strengthen our faith. Now we're required to act again.

Faith, action, more faith, more action. Growth demands more growth. This is "being on the path." Our faith focuses our awareness and energies, and our efforts produce results that strengthen our faith and our willingness to make further efforts.

IT DOESN'T GET EASIER

Following the path gets harder as we go. The deeper we penetrate into our personality, the more we see, the harder it is to let go of our attachments. The issues we deal with affect us more and more deeply, and the impact of working with them grows more and more overwhelming. The path narrows until it's like the edge of a razor.

We get trapped as we proceed, though. Once we've seen this process, what else is there for us to do? Once we've started growing, there's no going back. Even if we stop trying, the knowledge isn't forgotten. We're always on the path, even if we're starting all over again after having stopped moving forward for many years.

> *Come, come, whoever you are,*
> *Wanderer, worshipper, lover of leaving;*
> *Ours is not a caravan of despair.*
> *Come, even if you've broken your vows a thousand times.*
> *Come, come, yet again, come.*
> —Rumi

HOW TO HAVE FAITH

When you don't believe, no explanation is possible.
When you do believe, no explanation is necessary.
—Sign in front of the grotto at the National Shrine of the Grotto
of Our Lady of Lourdes, in Maryland

A lack of faith is one of the great spiritual crises of our time. Many people would like to have faith, but they don't. They don't want to pretend. They want the real thing, but they don't know how to get it. There's no rational explanation for faith, since there's ultimately no logical proof of God's existence. It isn't rational to have faith.

But having faith isn't irrational, either. It's nonrational, of a different order altogether. The traditional phrase "a leap of faith" describes the beginning of the process. We have to stop demanding rational reasons for faith, proof of the Absolute's existence. That's like trying to use a hammer to cut a piece of wood. Faith is a leap into a different space.

FAKE IT TILL YOU MAKE IT

A traditional Sufi saying contains an important clue on how to learn faith: "When you think of God, cry. But if you can't cry real tears, cry false ones, and God will make them real." We can focus our awareness on what we want to believe: on our conception of the Absolute or on the process of growth. We can act as if we believed in it with all our heart, with all our mind, and with all our strength. We will, after a while. Our sincere desire will open a space for the Divine Presence to come to us.

EXERCISES

1. Each day, spend a few minutes sitting calmly. Pretend that God is there with you. What would you say? How

would you feel? How would it affect you? Keep doing this. It's called "praying as if," or "practicing the presence."

2. Other parts of this book have suggested clarifying your values, specifying your financial goals, creating a budget, and taking the appropriate financial action to reach those goals. If you haven't done this yet, do it now.

Write out your financial goals, and start saving and investing so you can reach them. Invest appropriately: the longer the time frame, the more you'll want to focus on stocks rather than fixed-income investments such as certificates of deposit, government securities, and corporate or municipal bonds.

Make sure you've maximized your deductible contributions to your pension plan before doing other investing. When you do start investing, you'll want to use mutual funds for the diversification, professional management, and convenience they offer.

3. Learn the fundamentals of investing. Learn about the historical performance of different kinds of investments and the different risks involved in the short run and the long run. Learn about asset allocation and how to structure the appropriate portfolio for your particular needs.

Investments are like medications: they have specific purposes, they behave in certain ways when you use them, and they have certain side effects. Learn which investments are used for which purposes.

4. Don't let yourself be scared by others' lack of faith in themselves or in the future. Many people are ready to believe anything that confirms their preexisting fears. This attitude paralyzes them, preventing them from acting in

their own best interest. And there's always bad news around that they can use to confirm their fears. If you fall into their trap, you'll become just as fearful and paralyzed as they are.

CHAPTER TWELVE

CONCLUSION: WE'RE IN THE MONEY

If you've taken the ideas in this book seriously, you've started a process of great personal and spiritual growth. This book hasn't tried to convince you that a certain spiritual path or religious tradition is best. It *has* tried to inspire you to discover your unique spiritual path and to make progress along that path your ultimate life purpose. It's also tried to give you some tools to help you along your way.

Our experience of money can be one of those tools. By now we've seen how deeply our experience of money has penetrated our personality, and how powerful its associated patterns of belief and behavior are. As Henry Ford once said, "Money doesn't change men, it merely unmasks them." It shows us to ourselves.

Anything that reveals our inner workings is worth gold. As all the great spiritual guides and religious traditions teach, we stand in our own way, in between ourselves and the Divine Presence. Anything that gets us out of the way, that helps us make less of ourselves, is a treasure greater than any gold, silver, or precious gem. How fortunate we are that such treasure can be found all around us!

It's ironic that fool's gold can be a tool to use in the search for real gold, but it can. Throughout recorded history, human beings have created false gods. Money—and what it has come to mean—is only one of the latest false gods in this long tradition. History further shows that our hope for finding the truth lies in realizing an idol's falseness.

Why couldn't the path be easier? Because *this* is what we're here to learn! If human life has any purpose at all, it's to grow in awareness, to deepen one's consciousness until we come in touch with the universal consciousness that we call God.

In the Sufi tradition, there's a lovely saying about why the world was created, in which God says, "I was a hidden treasure, and I longed to be known, so I created the world that I might be known." This world is the place where God gains self-consciousness. That's the ultimate act of service a human being performs. Through us, the Divine Presence comes to know itself.

As we should know by now, money is no different from other parts of our lives. We can use our relationships as a mirror, our work as a mirror; in fact, we can use everything we think, say, and do as a way to see ourselves more clearly. Money is very important to us, however, and we tend to ignore it as a source of self-awareness, so it's been this book's intention to offer you a new tool for your spiritual work.

If you feel somewhat disillusioned—be happy! It would be worse to be stuck in illusory beliefs for the rest of your life. Many people live their whole lives in a fantasy world of their own creation. There's nothing we can do for them—until we've freed ourselves. We shouldn't feel dismayed or disturbed by this; it's just the way things are. What is important is our determination to use our experience of money, along with our experience of everything else in our lives, to grow personally and spiritually.

Each morning when we get up, we can take a vow: *This day will set me free a little bit more.* Write this on a piece of paper and tape it to your bathroom mirror where you can't miss seeing it. And you can write it ten times every morning to help you focus your intention for the day.

We can't control what happens out there in the world. We might like to, but we can't. All we have is what happens inside us, but that's all we need.

Yea, though I pass through the valley of the shadow of death,
I shall fear no evil, for Thou art with me.
—Twenty-third Psalm

Life is the valley of the shadow of death. The one thing we know for sure is that our time here is limited. But there's another great truth told by all religious traditions. God— however we define or describe that being, state of existence, or aspect of reality—is always as close to us as our jugular vein. As St. Francis of Assisi said, "What you are looking for is what is looking."

What other knowledge do we need? There are no esoteric secrets more powerful than the full realization of that truth. All the ancient and revered texts do nothing but talk about this. And there's no place better than where we are now to start realizing the truth. If there are things we think are holding us back, they are precisely what offer us the most knowledge and enhanced awareness of ourselves. What great king, robber baron, or billionaire has had any wealth greater than this?

We don't have to go anywhere or do anything to find our spiritual path. We can stay where we are, fulfill our material responsibilities, and experience the joy "that passeth all understanding."

We have the same opportunity to use money as a tool for encountering the Divine Presence in our lives whether we're rich, middle-class, or poor. We've got the same chance as anyone else to use our relationships, our work, and everything else in our lives as tools to help us encounter God. What can be taken from us or done to us that would make us unable to make use of this awareness? No one is standing in our way—except us.

Start now, have faith, pay attention, use your life as a mirror, be diligent, be grateful, surrender, and have fun.

SUGGESTED READING

Books

Bamford, Janet, et al. *Consumer Reports Moneybook*. Yonkers, N.Y.: Consumer Reports Books, 1992.

Brouwer, Kurt. *Mutual Funds: How to Invest With the Pros*. New York: John Wiley & Sons, 1988.

Bush, Lawrence, and Jeffrey Dekro. *Jews, Money and Social Responsibility*. Philadelphia: The Shefa Fund, 1993.

Ellis, Charles D. *Investment Policy: How to Win the Loser's Game*. Homewood, Ill.: Business One Irwin, 1987.

Givens, Charles. *More Wealth Without Risk*. New York: Simon & Schuster, 1991.

Harrington, John. *Investing with Your Conscience*. New York: John Wiley & Sons, 1992.

Hill, Napoleon. *Think and Grow Rich*. New York: Ballantine, 1960.

Hirsch, Michael D. *Multifund Investing*. Homewood, Ill.: Dow-Jones Irwin, 1987

———. *Mutual Fund Wealth Builder*. New York: HarperCollins, 1992.

Pond, Jonathan D. *1,001 Ways to Cut Your Expenses*. New York: Dell, 1991.

Quinn, Jane Bryant. *Making the Most of Your Money*. New York: Simon & Schuster, 1991.

Savage, Terry. *Terry Savage Talks Money*. Chicago: Dearborn Financial Publishing, 1990.

Dominguez, Joe, and Vicki Robin. *Your Money or Your Life.*
New York: Viking Penguin, 1992.

VandenBroeck, Goldian, ed. *Less Is More: The Art of
Voluntary Poverty.* Rochester, Vt.: Inner Traditions
International, 1991.

SOFTWARE

Andrew Tobias' Managing Your Money. Fairfield, Conn.:
MECA.

Money Magazine's Wealthbuilder. King of Prussia, Pa.: Reality
Technologies.

Quicken. Menlo Park, Calif.: Intuit.

Retire ASAP. Kirkland, Wash.: Calypso Software.

REFERENCES

Aurobindo, Sri. "The Role of Money," *Parabola 16* (Spring 1991).

Blau, Anne Kohn. *The Sex of the Dollar: Street-Smart Financial Planning for Women.* New York: Simon & Schuster, 1988.

Bolles, Richard. *What Color Is Your Parachute?* Berkeley: Ten Speed Press, 1991.

Bynner, Witter, trans. *The Way of Life According to Lao Tzu.* New York: Putnam, 1972.

Ram Dass. *Be Here Now.* San Cristobal, N.M.: Lama Foundation, 1971.

Dominguez, Joe. *Transforming Your Relationship with Money and Achieving Financial Independence.* (audiotape course). Seattle: New Road Map Foundation, 1986.

Feldman, Christina, and Jack Kornfield. *Stories of the Spirit, Stories of the Heart.* New York: HarperCollins, 1991.

Gibran, Kahlil. *The Prophet.* New York: Alfred A. Knopf, 1971.

Gurney, Kathleen. *Your Money Personality.* New York: Doubleday, 1988.

Hallowell, Edward M., M.D., and William J. Grace, Jr. *What Are You Worth?* New York: Weidenfeld & Nicolson, 1989.

Helminski, Camille, and Kabir Helminski. *Rumi: Daylight.* Putney, Vt.: Threshold Books, 1990.

Kaye, Yvonne, Ph.D. *Credit, Cash, and Co-Dependency.* Deerfield Beech, Fla.: Health Communications, Inc., 1991.

Lindgren, Henry Clay. *Great Expectations: The Psychology of Money.* Los Altos, Calif.: William Kaufman, Inc., 1980.

Mellan, Olivia. *Ten Days to Money Harmoney: A Guide for Individuals and Couples.* Washington, D.C.: Olivia Mellan & Associates, Inc., 1989.

Miller, Emmett. *Power Vision: Life Mastery Through Mental Imagery.* (audiotape) Chicago: Nightingale-Conant, 1987.

Needleman, Joseph. *Money and the Meaning of Life.* New York: Doubleday, 1992.

Phillips, Carole. *Money Talk: The Last Taboo.* New York: Arbor House, 1984.

Robbins, Lynn G. *Uncommon Cents.* Salt Lake City: Franklin International Institute, Inc., 1989.

Schumacher, E. F. *Good Work.* New York: Harper & Row, 1979.

———. *Small Is Beautiful.* New York: Harper & Row, 1973.

Schuon, Frithjof. *Understanding Islam.* London: George Allen and Unwin, 1965,

Zaleski, Phil. "The Test of Giving," *Parabola 16* (Spring 1991).